1000 Best
Wine Secrets

1000 Best Wine Secrets

CAROLYN HAMMOND

SOURCEBOOKS, INC.®
NAPERVILLE, ILLINOIS

Published by Sourcebooks, Inc.
P.O. Box 4410, Naperville, Illinois 60567-4410
(630) 961-3900
FAX: (630) 961-2168
www.sourcebooks.com

Library of Congress Cataloging-in-Publication Data
Hammond, Carolyn.
  1000 best wine secrets / Carolyn Hammond.
     p. cm.
  Includes index.
  ISBN-13: 978-1-4022-0808-9
  ISBN-10: 1-4022-0808-1
 1. Wine and wine making. I. Title. II. Title: One thousand best wine
secrets.

TP548.H228 2006
641.2'2—dc22

                                        2006020836

Printed and bound in Canada.
WC 10 9 8 7 6 5 4 3 2

For Geoffrey.

Contents

Acknowledgments

This book is not an island.

It was inspired by many others, most importantly the grape growers and winemakers who toil daily for the sheer love of producing pleasure in a glass—Philippe and Marcel Guigal, Charles Back, Marcelo Papa Cortesi, Alvaro Palacios, Clotilde Davenne, Jean-Baptiste Lecaillon, Nicholas Joly, Toby Barlow, John Hancock, and thousands more whose talents I've tasted.

Let me thank those who spend their days communicating the stories of the grapes, land, and people behind the wines and arranging tastings— Brigitte Batonnet, Hal Bibby, Jo Burzynska, David Churchill, Natasha Claxton, Michael Cox, John Derrick, Alison Dillon, Michael Donohue, Isidoro Fernandez-Valmayor, Jane Holland, Gladys Horiuchi, Sue Glasgow, Rob Green, Bill Gunn MW, Natalie Jeune, Peter Kelsall, Florence Laurent, Gérard Liger-Belair, Martine Lorson, Allison Lu, Angela Lyons, Stephen Marentette, Darren Meyers, Ian Mitchell, Giovanni Olivia, Sylvia Palamoudian, Sue Pike, Daryl Prefontaine, Dacotah Renneau, John Reynolds, Kelly Roberts, Jaimi Ruoho, Russell Sandham, Barbara Scalera, Camille Seghesio, Paul Sullivan, Elizabeth Vaughan, Chloe Wenban-Smith, Corrina Wilson, Jason Woodman, and Rebecca Yates-Campbell. Their support was invaluable.

And then there are my fellow wine writers whose steady stream of sentences broadens my view of the ever-expanding world of wine, particularly Jancis Robinson MW, Tim Atkin MW, Andrew Jefford, and Hugh Johnson, whose writings never fail to encourage me to dig a little deeper, uncork another bottle, and taste some more wine.

Perhaps most directly responsible for this book are Jacqueline Sach, my literary agent; Bethany Brown, my editor; and Russell, my spectacular husband, who always has faith in everything I do.

Introduction

"Wine is bottled poetry." Robert Louis Stevenson had it right. And like poetry, it reveals itself best when you're an active and sensitive participant. With wine, each bottle needs to be selected, uncorked, and tasted. It may be stored, chilled, and paired with food. You may choose to decant it. Or not. All with the hope your mouth will receive it gratefully. Joyfully.

This book is designed to help you get more pleasure from every bottle. The first two sections reveal secrets, such as how to establish what a wine will taste like by a quick glance at the label; how to know if a wine is ready to drink or will improve with cellaring; and how to pair wine with food so the union is greater than the sum of its parts. You'll learn when and why to decant or double decant and how to know if a wine is faulty—corked, past its best, or otherwise flawed. In short, sections one and two offer the means to magnifying your appreciation of wine.

Part three reveals the flavors of the world. It looks to the warm and spicy Cabernet-Shiraz blends from Australia, the plumply fruited Beaujolais, the swollen cherry Merlots from Chile, the balmy breath of Grenache-based reds from Rioja, and the cool strokes of summer captured in Loire valley whites. These reliable and undemanding wines are proof that pleasure doesn't have to be expensive or complicated. Since we sometimes yearn for more, this section also reveals the more complex styles.

Wines that take a little more effort. They may be more pricey and ask more of us in terms of understanding them and treating them well, but they usually repay us graciously, each sip coaxing more pleasure from the head and heart. Discover which celebrated plots of the Côte d'Or, Napa Valley, Bordeaux, Piedmont, and the Mosel Valley produce wines worth every penny and, if you're feeling a little more adventurous, where to turn for the best bottles of the Central Otago, the Willamette Valley, Ribera del Duero, or the Okanagon Valley.

These pages expose the better vineyards, growers, and winemakers from Italy to India, including the celebrated and shadowy heroes behind the bottles.

The fourth part of this book is a collection of trade secrets. This is where I've taken pleasure in debunking myths, noting the industry's most reliable sources of information, creating a lexicon of useful wine terms and jotted other useful bits and bobs for you to flip through with a glass of something delicious.

In short, this book is a list of 1000 wine secrets offered to you in friendship. So sit back, pour yourself a glass of your favorite tipple, and let me share with you some of what I know about wine.

Part One:

Selecting That Perfect Bottle

The best way to buy great wine is to know what you're looking for, and to be able to put it into words—whether you're talking with a merchant or a sommelier. It's easier to find an unoaked crisp white wine with restrained flavors of green apple than a fabulous dry white. The latter means a dozen different things to a dozen people, so the odds of being perfectly pleased are slim.

I cannot stress enough the importance of personal taste when choosing wine. The first chapter of this book reveals secrets to help you pinpoint your preferences, which are the foundation stones for much of the rest of this book. From there, you'll learn secrets of ordering wine in a restaurant, pairing food and wine, knowing when to drink it, and deciphering labels. These are the touchstones to selecting and appreciating that perfect bottle.

1.

Buying Great Wine

1. The best way to determine what a wine will taste like is by looking at the grape variety from which it's made. This is where the main flavor comes from. Wine made from Cabernet Sauvignon tastes like black currant, Chardonnay like citrus, Merlot like cherry, and so on. A wine takes on additional nuances depending on where the grapes were grown and the winemaking techniques used, but the fundamental flavor of the grape variety remains the same.

2. The chart below shows what the world's major red and white grape varieties taste like once they've been made into wine. Those in bold print are the most popular varieties.

Red Grape Varieties	Flavor
Anglianico	Tar and burnt cherry
Auxerrois	*See Malbec*
Baco Noir	Black forest fruits, leather, and spice
Barbera	Red plum and red cherry
Breton	*See Cabernet Franc*
Cabernet Franc	Ripe raspberry, pencil shavings, and herbs; also called Breton
Cabernet Sauvignon and often a hint of mint	Black currant, cedar, or eucalyptus
Canaiolo	Strawberry and leather
Cannonau	Herbs, blackberry, and spice
Carignan	Black plum and black pepper
Carménère	Cherry and red plum
Cencibel	*See Tempranillo*
Cinsault	Blueberry, blackberry, red meat
Corvina	Cherry and almonds
Cot	*See Malbec*
Dolcetto	Plum, mixed berries, and bitter almond
Dornfelder	Red bell pepper and mixed berries
Gamay	Ripe raspberry, strawberry, and often banana
Gamay Beaujolais	Raspberry; this grape is actually a clone of Pinot Noir
Garnacha	Very ripe mixed berries,

	meat, and black pepper; also called Grenache
Grenache	*See Garnacha*. White Grenache is a pink berry-scented wine made from this red grape
Grolleau	Mixed berries; also called Groslot
Groslot	*See Grolleau*
Lambrusco	Strawberry and cherry
Malbec	Blackberry, black plum, and dried fruit; also called Cot and Auxerrois
Merlot	Dark chocolate and cherry
Monastrell	Blackberry and game
Montepulciano	Blackberry and cherry
Mourvèdre	Blackberry, game, and leather
Napa Gamay	Mixed berries and violet; also called Valdiguié
Nebbiolo	Rose and tar
Petit Sirah	Red currant; not related to Syrah
Petit Verdot	Black pepper, mixed spices, and black currant
Pinotage	Black licorice and mixed berries
Pinot Noir	Ripe raspberry and canned strawberries when young; capable of changing dramatically when aged, taking on

	flavors of caramelized meat drippings, farm yard, and truffle
Portugieser	Mixed berries
Primivito	Blackberry, blueberry, and peppercorn; also called Zinfandel
Sangiovese	Cherry
Shiraz	Blackberry, black pepper, dark chocolate, and smoke; also called Syrah
Spätburgunder	*See Pinot Noir*
Syrah	*See Shiraz*
Tannat	Raspberry and leather
Tempranillo	Strawberry and dark chocolate
Teroldego	Mixed berries and tar
Tinta Borroca	Cherry and mushroom
Tinot Fino	*See Tempranillo*
Tinta Roriz	Mixed red berries and flowers
Touriga Nacional	Ripe berries and red roses
Trollinger	Red berries and flowers
Ull de Llebre	*See Tempranillo*
Valdiguié	*See Napa Gamay*
Zinfandel	*See Primivito*; White Zinfandel is a pink wine made from this red grape that tastes of ripe berries
<u>White Grape Varieties</u>	<u>Flavor</u>
Albariño	Granny Smith apple and herbs
Aligoté	Hints of peach and nuts

Auxerrois	Fairly neutral with hints of apple. Not to be confused with Auxerrois Gris from Alsace or the red grape Auxerrois from Cahors in France
Auxerrois Gris	*See Pinot Gris*
Bacchus	Flowers and Golden Delicious apple
Chardonnay	Mixed citrus and apple
Chasselas	Neutral with hints of green apple and peach
Chenin blanc	Flowers, honey, and moist straw
Clairette	Peach and melon
Clevner	*See Pinot Blanc*
Colombard	Lemon and peach
Cortese	Mineral and lime
Fiano	Hazelnut and flowers
Furmint	Apple and honey
Fumé Blanc	*See Sauvignon Blanc*
Gewürztraminer	Lychee and rose
Greco	Lime and herbs
Grüner Veltliner	Lime
Kerner	Lime, minerals, and herbs
Klevner	*See Pinot Blanc*
Macabeo	White flowers and nuts; also called Viura
Malvasia	Citrus, musk, and almond
Marsanne	Restrained pineapple, marzipan, and caramel
Moscatel	*See Muscat*
Moscato	*See Muscat*
Mauzac	Apple skin

Müller-Thurgau	White flowers and herbs
Muscadelle	Ripe grapes and flowers
Muscadet	Quite neutral with slight lemony nuance
Muscat	Ripe grape and orange; also called Moscato in Italy and Moscatel in Spain
Nuragus	Lemon
Parellada	Green apple and grapefruit
Pinot Blanc	Apple and ripe white peach; also called Clevner or Klevner
Pinot Grigio	Neutral aroma with very slight lemon, floral flavor; also called Pinot Gris in France, where it's harvested later and develops more flavor
Pinot Gris	Spiced peach; also called Auxerrois Gris and Tokay d'Alsace in Alsace, Ruländer in Germany, and Pinot Grigio in Italy. When grown in Italy as Pinot Grigio, it's harvested before developing pronounced flavors
Riesling	Lime, stones, and flowers; aged Riesling smells of gasoline
Rolle	Nuts, herbs, and citrus

Roussanne	Apricot
Ruländer	Spiced peach
Sauvignon Blanc	Lime, asparagus, and gooseberries; also called Fumé Blanc
Scheurebe	Grapefruit and peach
Sémillon	Creamy lemon curd
Seyval Blanc	Grapefruit
Silvaner	Quite neutral with restrained green apple. Also called Sylvaner
Sylvaner	*See Silvaner*
Tokay d'Alsace	*See Pinot Gris*
Torrontés	Peach and flowers
Trebbiano	Sour and very neutral with slight lemon notes; also called Ugni Blanc
Ugni Blanc	*See Trebbiano*
Verdejo	Sour lemon, herbs, and nuts
Verduzzo	Citrus, pineapple, and honey
Verdicchio	White flowers and hints of bitter almond
Vidal	Apricot and honey
Viura	*See Macabeo*
Viognier	Peach and pear
Xarel-lo	Flowers and apricot

3. Most wines are made from one or two grape varieties and, with very few exceptions, red grapes make red wine and white make white. Pink wine can be made by mixing wines made from red and white grapes, or from just red grape varieties.

4. Most wines name their grape varieties on their front or back labels. Those that don't are usually traditional wines from Europe labeled with the place they were made, such as Barolo, Chianti, or Bordeaux. You can learn what grapes are in these and other more classic wines by flipping to "Reavealing the Flavors of the World" in part 3 of this book.

5. As well as a characteristic flavor, each grape variety shows distinguishing levels of tannin and sourness—known as acidity. These elements influence how a wine tastes and whether it's to your liking. Nebbiolo, Malbec, and Cabernet Sauvignon make notably tannic wines, for instance, and Sauvignon Blanc, unoaked Chardonnay, and Grüner Veltliner make wines that are lemon-squirt sour. To some degree, these characteristics can be influenced by where the fruit is grown and the winemaking techniques used, but it's useful to learn your preferred level of tannin and acidity and which grapes produce wines that fit the bill. More about determining tannin and acidity can be found in chapter 6, "Tasting Wine Like a Pro," and part 3 of this book, "Flavors of the World."

6. If you're like me, your wine preferences vary with the weather, the seasons, and what you're eating. A sour white wine is a great refresher in the summer or with a spicy dish, while a robust red on a chilly day, perhaps with roasted meat, is most satisfying.

7. Sour wines tend to come from cooler climates. Countries further from the equator such as Austria, Germany, Canada, and Great Britain, as well as cool regions in hot countries such as the mountains of Chile, produce wines with more natural acidity or freshness.

8. If you like vanilla, search out wine aged in American oak. For aromas and flavors such as black and white pepper, cinnamon, and coffee, look for wine aged in French oak. Information on the type of oak used is often noted on back labels.

9. Better wines are fermented or matured in oak barrels rather than less costly oak chips, staves, or essence. If a wine's label uses more elusive phrases such as "oak maturation" or "oak influence" rather than the word "barrel," the winemaker has probably chosen one of the less expensive methods. Barrels create more integrated wood flavors.

10. Traditional Old World wines tend to be more restrained and less fruit-forward than New World wines. Some critics call New World wine alcoholic fruit juice, but it's very popular. The Old World includes the wine-growing regions of Europe that have been making wine for centuries. The New World refers to countries that began making and exporting large quantities of wine in the last one hundred years or so, such as North America, South America, and Australia.

11. Despite the tendency for the New World to make fruitier wines than the Old World, exceptions exist. Many New World producers now copy Old World wines at the higher end of the price spectrum. Meanwhile, the Old World is making inexpensive New World look-alikes—fruity wines that name grape varieties on the labels.

12. The best way to buy great wine is through a knowledgeable wine merchant. For merchants, especially those that are small and independent, there's no commercial place for mediocrity. They have to sell well to survive. This alone is sound reason to shop there. Once you find a great wine merchant, talk to him or her about what you like, what you don't like, and how much you're generally willing to spend. He or she will be tasting wines all the time and will be a source of valuable information.

13. It's important to remember that critics tend to taste for typicity as well as quality and preference. A critic might not like Beaujolais for instance, but will have tasted enough of them to tell whether one is a good quality version showing the clean, fresh, fruity character typical of the wine style. The point here is that high scores from a critic will mean nothing if you don't like the style of wine he or she is assessing.

14. Above all else, trust your own palate. Everyone's tasting experience is unique; a trusted critic can offer guidance, but rely on your own taste buds to decide if a wine is worth buying.

15. It has to be said that the power of the Internet has dethroned wine critics in some ways because so many passionate enthusiasts post their tasting notes. These, along with producer websites, make it as easy as a Google search to research wines before buying them.

16. When you find a wine you love, buy a few bottles and stash them in a cool place. You'll be glad you did. As well as some bottles you love, wines that are good to have around include a bottle of Champagne for when there's a cause to celebrate, a bottle of Beaujolais because it goes with almost any meal, and a bottle of dessert wine to enjoy as a treat with fresh fruit or salty cheese on a whim.

17. Heavily oaked whites can taste lovely and creamy at first blush but they tend to tire the palate after a glass or two.

18. Better wines are usually found in heavier bottles. This is a clue to quality.

19. A good way to ensure that a wine is of a fairly high standard is to look at the name of the producer. When you buy from a reputable producer, you can be fairly sure the wine won't let you down. Your wine merchant can help you learn the names of a few trusted producers in your favorite wine regions, as can this book.

20. Learn about and taste regional varieties, not just those from more popular international grapes. Great value for the money lies here. Reading part 3 of this book, "Revealing Flavors of the World," will set you off in the right direction.

21. Remember value for money is subjective. Much depends on things like the depth of your pocket and your personal taste.

22. The bottle, label, closure, capsule, carton, distribution costs, wholesale, and retail margins, as well as applicable duties and taxes, are all fixed costs so, the more you pay for a bottle, the more wine you're actually getting for your buck.

23. Larger companies tend to economize wherever possible so you usually get what you pay for, but no more. Underpriced wines tend to come from smaller producers driven by a fervent passion to produce the best quality wine for the sheer love of it. They to compete on quality because they often lack the economies of scale to compete on price. Where do you find these gems? Through smaller wine merchants who know the producers personally, revere their wines, and understand the good value they offer. Today, small producers often turn to independent merchants and restaurants to sell their wines because they often simply cannot afford the steep listing fees and promotional costs required by supermarkets and larger retailers, nor can they provide the volumes demanded there.

24. Big brands have their merits. In the best cases, they deliver consistency and good value for the money—crowd-pleasers if you will. They are also easy to find because they're often stocked at major stores and they're generally quite easy to like even if most won't make you ponder their nuances and wax lyrically. Some are better than others though. As always, look to reliable producers for the best bottles.

25. As the world becomes awash with generic, mass-produced wines, the pendulum is starting to swing back. A demand for artisanl wine is gathering pace, giving rise to hundreds if not thousands of quality-minded producers tending their vines and winemaking with such care, passion, and respect, it's hard not to taste the difference in the glass.

26. Although organic wines don't *always* taste better than their more conventional counterparts, they offer two unique pleasure doses—knowing you aren't putting extra chemicals in your body and knowing you, in a small way, are helping save the planet.

27. Almost every region is now producing organic wines. However, not all makers market themselves as such. Some fear being associated with what may be a fad, and others want the freedom to treat vines when necessary.

28. Some wine styles such as Pinot Noir are more expensive to make, which can mean the price is often higher than that of, say, Chardonnay, which is easier to produce.

29. Is there really a discernable difference between a $10 bottle and a $50 bottle? The answer is, absolutely. Generally, the more expensive wine will be more refined; made from better quality grapes; and have more concentration, complexity, and length. The thing to remember though, is the $50 wine may not be ready to drink, and so the $10 bottle will offer more immediate drinking pleasure. Also, at each price point, the playing field is notoriously uneven, so some $10 bottles are much better than other $10 ones.

30. Learning the main facts about wine will help you buy better wine and earn you a more rewarding relationship with your merchant. Finding out the basics requires a bit of homework, but it pays off. To get you started, read chapter 29, "Learning More about Wine."

31. The best producers are those that control the winemaking process from vineyard to cellar, and are fastidious about every little step.

32. Respecting diversity in wine is critical to appreciation. Don't compare a classed growth Bordeaux to a premium Australian Cabernet Sauvignon, tempting though it may be. They differ stylistically.

33. Auction houses are good places to get bargains on midrange wines, costing $350–$1,500 per case.

34. To get the best wine you can at the best prices, go to www.wine-searcher.com. This website lets you search for a wine by name, vintage, and location, telling you who stocks the wine in what country and at what price. It's a great site for wine drinkers, though merchants no doubt loathe its transparency. If you can't find a particular bottle on this website, ask your local wine retailer to stock it.

35. Use vintage guides as just that—a guide. A vintage rating is a sweeping generalization and there are always exceptions to the year's rating.

36. In your quest for that perfect bottle, remember that time, place, mood, company, and food all influence how much you enjoy it—almost as much as what is actually in the bottle.

37. The best way to make a good wine great and a great wine memorable is to drink it with someone with whom you're in love.

38. Although all of the secrets listed above are true, none are the truth. The truth is wine appreciation starts and ends with your connection with the wine and your respect for the fruit, earth, and sun that goes into it.

2.

Ordering Wine in a Restaurant

39. Before you order wine, ask the other diners if they would prefer red or white instead of asking them what they're ordering. Many people don't go by the rules of red with meat, white with chicken, and so forth, so it's best to cut to the chase and find out what they want to drink. Once you've narrowed it down by color, you're on your way to finding something agreeable to all.

40. Scan the prices and decide on an amount you're willing to spend on a bottle. Keep your expectations realistic. If you're paying about $25 for a bottle, don't expect it to be a deeply complex wine with great length. At best, you'll get something that shows clean fruit expression, and is pleasant to drink for that price.

41. Don't assume all the wines on the list are ready to drink. This means, if there is a $100 red Barolo from a recent vintage, you might find it's a glass full of unimpressive hard work because it will be too tannic—a stoic, impervious, unresolved wine that's completely unwilling to befriend you. Barolos generally don't provide pleasurable drinking until about ten years after their vintage date, and they certainly don't take kindly to impatience.

42. A good rule is, if you're considering a wine that's over $50 and it is under five years old, ask the sommelier or on-site wine expert if the wine is ready to drink.

43. If there's no sommelier available, ask the waiters your wine questions. They should know the wines they're serving. If not, ask to talk to the person in charge of buying the wines—often the owner or manager. That person will be the on-site wine expert. Don't be shy. These people are there to help you enjoy your meal.

44. The best question to ask a sommelier is: What are the best two red or white wines in the [fill in your price] range? Stating your price range is critical because it creates a framework. Then, ask for a description of the recommended wines. This method taps a sommelier's expertise quickly and effectively.

45. If the on-site wine expert recommends something unusual, consider the suggestion carefully. Ask why he or she is enthusiastic about that wine and, when you can, give it a whirl. An insider generally has a better idea of what tastes particularly delicious on the list.

46. Drink the best wines you can afford at home and more local, less expensive bottles when dining out. This saves you paying fat restaurant markups on great bottles.

47. If your dining party is having courses, consider ordering one wine for the aperitif and perhaps the first course, and one or more wines for the courses that follow. Expecting a wine to wear too many hats leads to trouble. And try to remember that the first bottle should always be lighter in body or color than the later wines.

48. Just because the menu says it is Champagne doesn't mean it's the real deal. When in doubt, look at the country and region where it is made. New World countries produce sparkling wines and label them Champagne despite the fact that only wine produced in the region of France called Champagne is true to its name. And there is a world of difference in the real stuff and the impostors. Real Champagne typically tastes something like cooked apples, toast, and butter pastry.

49. Once you've chosen a wine on the menu, it should be brought to you unopened to view the label. Check the name of the wine and the year of vintage to confirm they match what you ordered. Once you give the nod, the waiter will open it and pour you a tasting measure. The idea here is not for you to taste it to see if you like it; it is to approve the quality of the wine—in other words, make sure it is not flawed. So, check to make sure the wine is clear rather than hazy, smells fresh and like wine instead of musty or otherwise nasty, and tastes equally clean. Once these things are confirmed, you can give the nod again and the waiter should fill the other diners' glasses and then yours.

50. Many restaurants will let you bring your own bottle and charge you a corkage fee, which is a surcharge to cover the privilege of drinking your own wine on the premises. Bringing your own bottle can be a good idea if you have a special wine with which to surprise your dining companion, perhaps from an older vintage. Bringing your own bottle of inexpensive wine doesn't usually make sense because the corkage fee usually exceeds the cost of the restaurant's markup on lower priced bottles. Don't forget to call ahead to ensure the establishment offers guests this option.

3.

Pairing Food and Wine

51. When pairing food and wine, body not color matters most. Body is the weight of the wine in your mouth and corresponds closely with alcohol level. Fuller bodied wines such as Cabernet Sauvignon, Barolo, and Syrah all go well with heavier dishes such as roasted meats, while lighter wines such as German Riesling, Pinot Blanc, and Beaujolais pair best with lighter fare such as salads.

52. Don't follow rules too strictly when pairing food and wine. Instead, drink what you like with your meals. Just try to refrain from major errors of judgment such as annihilating a delicate poached fish dish by pairing it with a heavy red, such as a big Australian Shiraz.

53. In the Old World especially, regional wines are made to compliment local fare. On the eastern seaboard of Italy for instance, the locals pair freshly caught fish and seafood with Verdicchio, the restrained white wine made in the area. Following suit makes good gastronomical sense.

54. Although Champagne is traditionally served with cake at weddings, it's a dubious match. Champagne tastes searingly sour when you pair it with very sweet food. It's best served on its own or with salty or savory foods.

55. Champagne is a wine, not just a celebratory tipple. It works marvelously as an aperitif, a first course accompaniment, or both. Bubbly has the refreshing tartness to freshen the palate, making it a good wine with which to whet the appetite, and its toasty, biscuity flavors makes it a lovely match for fresh salads, seafood, or even a plate of French fries. It's a classic match to sautéed mushrooms.

56. The best wines to pair with seafood include: Muscadet, Verdicchio, Chablis, and Champagne. All of these wines are delicate, restrained, and perfect with fish.

57. Salads dressed with lemon-based dressings are less likely to ruin the balance of an accompanying fine wine than those made with vinegar.

58. If you use a certain wine in a stew, drink the same one with the final dish. This ties the flavors together and creates harmony.

59. The French pair Alsacean Gewurztraminer with Munster, a cheese that has been made in Alsace since the Middle Ages originally by monks. Munster is a pungent cheese often eaten with baked potatoes and finely chopped onions, and pairs well with the rich, rose petal scent and full-body of Gewurztraminer wine.

60. Look for smoky wines to pair with grilled foods. Australian Shiraz, South African Pinotage, or reds from the Northern Rhône region of France such as Hermitage and Crozes Hermitage spring to mind.

61. Red wine can make fish taste metallic. This happens when iodine in fish meets tannin in red wine. To minimize the effect, choose red wines low in tannin such as Beaujolais or Merlot, or play it safe and serve white or rosé.

62. Sour wines such as those made from Pinot Noir, Sauvignon Blanc, or unoaked Chardonnay pair well with fattier foods because the tartness of the wine cuts the richness of the food.

63. Although cheese is usually paired with red wine, don't discount whites. A milky goat's cheese marries beautifully with the herbaceousness of Sauvignon Blanc; the lemony, toasty flavors of white Burgundy are excellent with the pungent richness of Parmesan Reggiano; and the sweetness of Sauternes absolutely salutes the salty tang of Roquefort.

64. If you're planning a menu, don't discount the idea of a sweet wine paired with fresh fruit instead of a dessert. A great match is a very good quality Sauternes, Barsac, or Tokaji Aszú with fresh, ripe peaches tossed with a squirt of lemon and a drizzle of honey.

65. If you plan to pair sweet wine with dessert, the food should be less sweet than the wine. If not, the wine will taste searingly sour and out of balance. And if the wine is of particularly high quality, stick with a simple dessert of either fresh fruit or custard.

66. Look to the flavors in a wine when pairing it with food. Sauvignon Blanc smells of asparagus so it's a great match for this vegetable. Similarly, the crushed red berry flavors of a young Pinot Noir goes well with turkey in much the same way cranberry sauce is a traditional accompaniment to this bird.

67. When you're serving an aged wine of good quality and expecting complexity, don't pair it with fancy food. Choose something simply prepared to ensure the wine isn't upstaged. If you're uncorking a well-aged Bordeaux blend such as Opus One from Napa, it would be better paired with a simple roasted prime rib of beef, potatoes, and steamed green beans than, say, a root vegetable and pear ragout with venison crepes.

68. Spicy foods such as Thai or Caribbean dishes often go very well with off-dry wines such as Californian White Zinfandel or halbtrocken German Riesling, which refresh the palate. These wines are slightly sweet but also tend to have fairly high levels of acidity that make you salivate when you drink them, creating a cooling effect in your mouth.

69. Sour wines and salty foods work well together. This means that you should look to crisp, refreshing wines such as Pinot Blanc or Silvaner to serve as aperitifs with salted finger foods. Great pre-meal standbys include Champagne with salted popcorn or potato chips, Fino Sherry with briny olives, and Muscadet with roasted salted cashew nuts.

70. When thinking about wine and food pairing, remember to match the strongest flavor in the dish to the wine. This dominant flavor may well be the sauce. A traditional pesto penne works very well with the herb and nut flavors of a Spanish Verdejo for instance.

71. If you're serving hors d'oeuvres outdoors in the summer, I can't think of a better match than a good quality, well-chilled rosé. In fact, rosé is frequently the wine selection of choice in Spain or France when dining al fresco in the summer. Not a selection to shy away from when patio season rolls around.

72. Tannins and protein are a winning combination. Wine tannins are attracted to proteins so, without getting too technical, a tannic wine will feel silky and full of fruit when consumed with meats and cheeses.

73. For those willing to splash out on the art of food and wine pairing, there's always Alain Senderens' three-star Michelin restaurant, Lucas Carton, in the 8th arrondissement of Paris. Monsieur Senderens is a veteran French chef who crafts dishes to match the texture, density, and aromas of chosen wines. Then, he offers diners a menu matched to wines served by the glass. The results are said to be magical. Visit www.lucascarton.com to learn more.

4.

Knowing When to Drink It

74. A good rule of thumb is, if the wine retails for less than $25, it's probably ready to drink. Wines above this price point are usually made with better quality grapes grown in better conditions, both of which tend to push the price up. With quality often comes aging potential. Remember, the vast majority of wines are ready to drink upon bottling.

75. Knowing when to drink a wine depends on your ability to detect the fruit concentration, tannin, acidity, and alcohol, and the balance of these four elements. Fruit concentration and tannin diminish as wine ages, while acidity and alcohol remain constant. So, a wine with more fruit and tannin than acidity and alcohol can improve with age.

76. When fruit concentration and tannin are in balance with acidity and alcohol, a wine is ready to drink. Once these elements are balanced, a wine will stay that way—or "keep"—for a period of time, the length of which varies.

77. Building on the last couple of secrets, fruit concentration is perceived mid-palate as flavor intensity. Tannins are felt around the gums as a drying sensation, much like the sensation of drinking strong black tea. Acidity is detected as sourness felt on the sides of the tongue making you salivate. And alcohol is felt as heat on the back of the palate, particularly after swallowing.

78. Knowing when an ageworthy wine is ready to drink is fairly subjective. Some people like their wines youthful, uncomplicated, and fresh tasting, while others prefer the more subtle levels of complexity that come with maturity.

79. Some grape varieties keep better than others and thus age more gracefully. A few reds that tend to age well are Cabernet Sauvignon, Nebbiolo (the grape of Barolo and Barbaresco wines), and Pinot Noir. Gamay and Cabernet Franc on the other hand are notoriously best drank young.

80. Whites generally don't age as well as reds because they lack tannin. Tannin present in red wine is a natural preservative.

81. Some white wines can improve with time in bottle, particularly those made from Riesling, Pinot Gris, and Chardonnay grapes, as long as they've been made well and have sufficient concentrations of fruit.

82. Champagne can age for decades. Vintage Champagne, which is usually made from the best fruit of the best years, has the most potential to improve in bottle. Look to better quality producers for stuff to lie down.

83. It is sometimes difficult to distinguish low quality wine that's harsh tasting from that which is high quality but not ready to drink. Both will have chewy tannins and frankly will be unpleasant to drink. One clue can be the price. But the most accurate way to tell is by judging the balance of the wine yourself. A low quality wine will show low fruit concentration relative to the tannins, acidity, and alcohol, while a high quality one will be comparatively rich in fruit.

84. Wines with long-term aging potential tend to require a seasoned palate to predict the number of years they will age. Top quality Bordeaux wines, for instance, are made to age for as many as fifty years. It takes a lot of tasting to make such predictions and, given the price of these wines, which can run into thousands of dollars per bottle, you don't want to uncork one to find out it's not ready. So, my advice to you is to look to your merchant or other experts' published drinking times for these wines, and use these windows as starting points.

85. Once you're fairly familiar with the method of judging if a wine is ready to drink, start practicing with wines in your cellar. Buy a fairly inexpensive case that isn't ready to drink that you're merchant says will age for at least five years. Then, in five years, taste a bottle. Note your thoughts on the balance and flavors, then decide when to uncork another. That's where aging wine starts to get fun.

86. The benefit of cellaring a wine made to age is that it develops layers of aromas and flavors. The aroma of an aged wine is called its bouquet.

87. Wines in magnum age about one and a half times as long as the same wine in a normal sized wine bottle. Wines in half bottles age more quickly than regular bottles of the same wine—in about two-thirds the time.

88. When you buy older vintages, you're paying for someone else's cellaring time and space. Buying young wine meant for aging and storing it yourself is a much better bargain as long as you can keep from raiding your cellar.

89. Sherry does not improve with time in the bottle and should be drank as soon after bottling as possible.

90. Sherry should be drank within about a week of opening a bottle. Dryer styles of Sherry such as Fino and Manzanilla deteriorate quickest.

91. Vintage Port improves with bottle age. Meanwhile, Crusted, Late Bottled Vintage, and Tawny Port styles are not meant for aging in bottle, so drink up.

92. All Port except for finer Tawnies should be drank within about a week of opening a bottle, much like Sherry. Fine Tawny Port can last up to a few weeks after uncorking.

93. One fortified wine that can stay fresh almost indefinitely after it has been uncorked is Madeira, which comes from the island of the same name about four hundred miles off the coast of Morocco. This fortified wine tastes of caramel and nuts, and comes in styles ranging from very sweet to dry. The reason it can stay fresh is because of the way it's made. It's the only wine in the world that is exposed to heat for months, if not years. This process gently cooks the wine, creating a characteristic dark color, rich tangy flavor, and almost indestructible nature.

94. Wine meant to be consumed young can start to lose its fresh, fruity appeal within about a year or so of being bottled, so opt for recent vintages when buying relatively inexpensive wines and consume them quickly. This is a particularly good rule to follow when buying pink and white wines because they deteriorate faster than reds.

95. Rosé wines don't generally improve with age. Always drink these young.

96. Beaujolais Nouveau—that fruity red from southern Burgundy made from Gamay grapes—should be drank by the May of the year after its vintage date.

5.

Reading the Label

97. A quick glance at the label will show if a wine is light-, medium-, or full-bodied because its body corresponds closely with its alcohol level. Light-bodied wines have less than 12 percent alcohol by volume (ABV); medium-bodied wines show 12–13 percent; and full-bodied wines exceed 13 percent. Californian Zinfandel immediately comes to mind as an example of a very full-bodied red wine often exceeding 14 percent, while German Riesling is usually quite light at around 9 percent ABV.

98. Most New World wines and an increasing number of those from the Old World name grapes on labels now, which is the quickest way to tell what a wine will taste like.

99. Wines from the United States are often labeled as regional wines from Europe, such as Burgundy, Claret, Chablis, Champagne, Chianti, Hock, Malaga, Marsala, Madeira, Moselle, Port, Rhine, Sauternes, Sherry, and Tokay. To ensure the wine is authentic, look for the country of origin, which also must appear on the label somewhere.

100. An agreement made in September 2005 between the U.S. and the EU will soon prevent the U.S. from using so-called semi-generic names such as Burgundy, Claret, and Chablis on new products. The restriction will not apply to existing impostors.

Part Two:

Tasting and Serving Wine

Selecting a great bottle only takes you halfway to drinking well. Fusing that swirl, mighty whiff, sip, and swallow with the more cerebral pleasures of tasting critically and serving properly takes you the rest of the way. Tasting with an eye for balance and quality gives you the language to talk about why you like a wine or not. You move from appreciating aromas and flavors to understanding the mouthfeel, structure, and harmony of a wine, and learning why these elements matter. With this wisdom, you can tell when a wine is flawed and, if it is, return it with confidence. And because wine is inherently social, the chapters that follow offer pointers to serving wine with panache.

Part Two

Tasting and Serving Wine

6.

Tasting Wine Like a Pro

101. The two things professional wine tasters look for when tasting a wine are its quality (low to high) and its level of maturity (meaning whether it's past its prime, in perfect drinking condition, or would improve in bottle). Age and maturity are different things. Age is the length of time a wine has been in existence, as determined by a quick glance at its vintage date, while maturity is a judgment call gauging its prime drinking time.

102. A wine's appearance in the glass reveals clues to its overall quality and maturity. The best way to look at a glass of wine is in bright light against a white background. Standing by a window with a sheet of plain paper or a white napkin behind the glass does the trick. Does it appear clear? This is the first indication of quality. Wine should be clear.

103. As well as clarity, the brightness of a wine matters. A wine can range from glossy and radiant to downright dull. Brilliance in the glass can indicate high acidity levels, as well as youth and vigor. Conversely, very dull wine is usually past its best, particularly if it has an orange hue.

104. Brightness can also indicate certain winemaking methods. If a wine is star-bright it has likely been ruthlessly filtered to remove the tiniest particles, which is a controversial practice. Critics argue it removes flavor, while proponents like the way it clarifies and stabilizes a wine, ensuring it stays clear. Unfiltered wine should appear clear in the glass but slightly dull.

105. The color of wine where it meets the glass, which is called the rim, is the best clue to a wine's maturity. As white wine matures, the rim turns from watery to golden and as red wine matures, the rim moves through a range of colors starting with purple, moving to ruby, russet, brick, and finally brown.

106. The traces of wine known as legs or tears left on the insides of the glass after giving it a swirl shows the alcohol and sweetness levels in a wine. If you see obvious legs, take notice and expect fairly high levels of alcohol or sugar on the palate.

107. The most important organ in tasting is not the tongue. It's the nose. Olfactory glands are far more sensitive than taste buds. If you don't believe me, try tasting something with a stuffy nose. So always remember to get your nose right in the glass and take a whiff before you take a sip. It improves your tasting experience immensely.

108. To nose a wine, which is winespeak for smelling it, give the glass a good swirl to encourage the aromas to vaporize. Then, take a good whiff. Some tasters feel one nostril is better than the other and tilt one side of their nose into the glass.

109. Wine should smell clean. When nosing the wine, look out for musty aromas. These odors generally indicate flaws or simply poor winery hygiene—neither of which is particularly appealing. More on this in chapter 8, "Detecting Faulty Wine and Sending It Back."

110. Some wines will seem to have no aroma, which is referred to as a "closed nose." This can happen at various points in a wine's evolution, and is not a flaw. Also, while certain grape varieties are very perfumed, such as Sauvignon Blanc, others are naturally restrained, such as wines made from Trebbiano.

111. The third thing to look for on the nose is aroma. It gives you a clue as to what grape the wine is made from, as well as the wine's quality level, age, and maturity. More complexity on the nose usually means the wine is of better quality, perhaps has some age, and is further along on its maturity continuum.

112. Primary aromas come from the grapes themselves, such as violets and roses, green pepper, and so forth. Secondary aromas come from the winemaking process. Strawberry, apple, black currant, banana, pineapple, wild berries, bread, and butter for instance arise from the fermentation process while toast, vanilla, and spice aromas come from oak aging. Bottle age creates tertiary aromas such as game, leather, tobacco, tar, mushroom, and dried flowers.

113. After you've looked at and smelled the wine, it's time to take a swig and swish it around so it touches every area of the tongue. Each part of this organ detects a specific sensation—sweetness, sourness, bitterness, and so on.

114. Sweetness is felt on the tip of the tongue. Paying attention to this part of the tongue when you taste a wine helps detect sugar levels—from bone dry to lusciously sweet. Judging sugar levels takes practice because other elements in wine—namely acidity and fruit intensity—hide sugar. This is probably why so many people think dry and drink sweet.

115. Sourness, known technically as acidity, is felt on the sides of the tongue. While some wine styles and varieties are more sour than others, all wines should have some acidity, which cleanses the palate by causing you to salivate. A wine with relatively high levels of sourness is often referred to as crisp or refreshing, while a wine with low acidity is called flabby.

116. For a wine high in sugar to be pleasant to drink, it must be equally high in acidity. This balance is critical because, without it, you wouldn't want to drink more than a sip or two. The wine would seem cloying.

117. Tannins are the astringent compounds found in skins, pips, and stems of grapes, and these parts are left in contact with fermenting juice when making red wine. This is why tannins are generally only found in red wines. In white winemaking, only the juice of grapes is fermented. Tannin is also found in oak, so occasionally white wines can have a bit of delicate tannin from oak aging.

118. Tannins are felt as a drying sensation around the gums and give a wine structure. Structure lets the wine age, keep, and stand up to food. You also notice tannins in overly steeped black tea and walnut skins.

119. Tannins differ. Ripe ones taste velvety while unripe ones taste rather stalky. Think of the difference between eating a well-ripened piece of fruit and one that's still a little green. It is fashionable today in regions such as California to let grapes hang on the vine longer than usual to ripen the tannins completely and eliminate all green flavors. Other regions such as the Loire in France appreciate the added nuance of a little unripe tannin in a red wine.

120. Fruit intensity—also called fruit concentration or extract—should be in balance with the levels of tannin and acidity. Fruit intensity is felt mid-palate, where tactile sensations are perceived.

121. Complexity is one of the earmarks of a good quality wine and can seem to suggest fruit, vegetables, minerals, animals, flowers, wood, spices, herbs, and empyreumatic aromas such as smoke, toast, caramel, and roasted foods.

122. Alcohol level is felt as heat on the back of the palate after you swallow or spit the wine. The alcohol is in balance if it doesn't stand out. You actually shouldn't taste the alcohol if the wine is balanced. Wine that is too old and hence lost its fruit, or has been produced in a very hot year, can be too high in alcohol. Not a nice drinking experience.

123. After you swallow, count one-steamboat, two-steamboat, three-steamboat, and so on until you can't taste the wine any more. The longer the length, the better the wine.

124. After tasting a wine methodically, you can determine if a wine is balanced, meaning one element doesn't overpower any of the others. If one element does stand out—such as tartness—consider the wine's inherent style. A Sancerre, for instance, should show relatively high acidity and a Barolo should display relatively high tannins.

125. Once you've tasted the wine and considered its elements, you are in a position to accurately gauge its maturity. Is it too young, ready to drink, or past its best? Knowing fruit concentration and, in red wines, tannin diminish as wine ages and acidity and alcohol remain the same, wines with more fruit and tannin than acidity and alcohol will improve with age. When fruit concentration and tannin are in balance with acidity and alcohol, it is ready to drink.

126. Balance, concentration, complexity, and length are the cornerstones of quality wine. Couple this fact with the price and you can determine if a wine delivers good value for the money.

127. An easy way to remember how to taste wine like a pro is to follow the three senses from the top of your face down—eyes to look, nose to smell, and mouth to taste.

128. When you find a wine you like, jot down some tasting notes to remember it. Is it reminiscent of cinnamon, cashew, smoke, tar, cigars, lilac, or thyme? Does it strike you as brooding, sassy, edgy, harmonious, elegant, mighty, or seductive? Log your impressions and jog your memory.

7.

Serving Wine Like a Pro

129. When serving several wines, pour white and rosé before red, younger bottles before older vintages, and dryer styles before sweeter ones.

130. Chilling wine is a good way to improve the taste of lesser quality wine. Chilling masks imperfections such as searing sourness, lack of complexity, or too little fruit. Conversely, over-chilling very good wine hides the subtle nuances of flavor that makes it interesting and pleasurable.

131. Serving temperature for all wine is rather important. Most white wines tend to taste best served a bit warmer than straight out of the fridge, where the temperatures are usually below a flavor-masking 41°F. The best route is to chill a white wine in the fridge and remove it about ten minutes or so before serving to let the wine warm up a bit. Serve finer white wines, such as Burgundy, a few degrees warmer still to bring out their myriad of aromas and flavors.

132. Red wines taste best a little cooler than room temperature—between about 57°F and 65°F—with lighter-bodied reds served near the cooler end of the range and fuller-bodied ones toward the warmer end.

133. Glasses are important. Riedel is a brand of crystal glasses that the trade often uses for professional tastings because they can enhance wines. Riedel matches glass shapes to various styles of wine to best effect and they do work, but buying the full range might be excessive. The company's glassmaker Georg Riedel has designed more than one hundred glasses. Unless you only drink a certain style of wine regularly, I would recommend a set of the Bordeaux Grand Cru glasses for drinking red wine and a set of Chablis (Chardonnay) for drinking white, as well as a set of vintage Champagne flutes for bubblies—all of which are in the Sommeliers Series.

134. If you choose not to invest in Riedel, you can still enhance a wine by serving it in a glass with a smaller rim to bowl ratio to capture the aroma of the wine.

135. There are two reasons to decant a wine—to separate the wine from the sediment and to aerate it. Red wine with significant bottle age throws a sediment, so it's best to decant it. And almost all wines—particularly full-bodied reds—benefit from aeration. The exception is very old ones that need quite gentle decanting to separate the wine from its sediment, but can lose character if exposed to too much air.

136. Different decanter styles exist for different wines. Young wines need more oxygen to open up than old wines, so a broad-bottomed decanter is best, giving the wine a larger surface area to be in contact with the air. Old wines on the other hand are more fragile, so taller, slimmer decanters are best, exposing less wine to the air yet offering means to separate the wine from the sediment.

137. To prepare an old wine for decanting to separate it from sediment, gently stand it upright for a couple of days to let the solids collect at the base of the bottle. Then, peer through the glass with a light source behind the bottle to ensure it's settled well.

138. You don't need any fancy glassware to decant. A clean funnel and a clean, empty wine bottle does the trick in a pinch. Just slowly pour the wine from one bottle to the next. Using a beautiful decanter is arguably more appropriate for certain occasions.

139. Serve old wines immediately after decanting as not to lose fragile aromas and flavors.

140. A very full-bodied, younger red wine often benefits from double decanting, which involves decanting the wine from its original bottle to another vessel and then back again into the bottle. This aerates the wine more than a single decant.

8.

Detecting Faulty Wine and Sending It Back

141. The first means of detecting a faulty wine is with the eyes. Hazy or cloudy wine usually suggests a fault from bacterial contamination, but it can also mean disturbed sediment in a red wine with bottle age. If the haze is due to a flaw, the nose and flavor of the wine will be off, smelling either musty or overly yeasty.

142. Sugar-like crystals at the bottom of a glass of white wine do not indicate a flaw. This deposit is tartaric acid, which is found naturally in grapes and does not compromise the quality of a wine. These crystals are often caused simply from the wine being chilled after fermentation. It might also interest you to know that the cooking ingredient, cream of tartar, is made from the build up of tartaric acid scraped from the inside of used wine vats.

143. Small bubbles in a glass of still wine can mean one of two things: either the wine is flawed because it has refermented spontaneously in the bottle, which usually isn't good and the wine will have a rather strong aroma of apples and yeast, or the producer deliberately left some carbon dioxide in the bottle to help keep it fresh. In the latter case, you wouldn't find the strong yeasty aroma and there would be no need to worry.

144. Many wine faults are detected on the nose, and confirmed on the palate. The most common one is cork taint now formally called TCA, short for 2, 4, 6 Trichloroanisole, because it's found in all sorts of things from wood to tap water. If a wine is tainted with TCA or "corked" as they say, it will range from smelling like musty, old, wet socks to simply seeming stripped of its fruit aromas. Be wary of attributing a wine with lack of fruit to TCA though because this can come from a lot of things. To confirm TCA as the cause, look for the telltale musty smell. And then return the bottle.

145. TCA is more evident in sparkling wines than still ones because the carbon dioxide, which gives the wine its bubbles, also makes the taint compounds vaporize, making it more apparent in the aroma.

146. If you detect the smell of bandages, you're probably finding Brettanomyces, known as Brett, which is a wild yeast that can get into wine. This fault is thought to be on a steep rise because Brettanomyces proliferates in wine that is ripe, highly extracted, and relatively high in alcohol—an increasingly popular style of wine. Although strictly speaking, Brett is a wine flaw, most critics agree a bit of Brett on the nose and palate can enhance the overall flavor of the wine by adding an interesting nuance. Brett is often confused with the gamey characteristics of the Mourvèdre grape, which is found in many Rhône red wines.

147. Is there an unmistakable scent of geraniums wafting from your glass? This is also a wine fault caused by a chemical reaction in wine that had potassium sorbate added and has undergone malolactic fermentation during winemaking.

148. If you detect an aroma of rotten eggs on the nose, be sure, this is a wine fault. It is hydrogen sulphide you smell, which should have been thoroughly removed at the winery. However, dropping a copper coin in a glass of wine displaying this fault will remove the hydrogen sulphide.

149. Vinegary aromas mean a wine is past its best, has been open too long, or has been overly exposed to oxygen.

150. If a wine smells like a recently struck match, it has too much free sulphur swimming around in it and the wine is faulty.

151. A smell of varnish, glue, or nail polish remover suggests a fault due to the presence of ethyl acetate in the wine. This is not a chemical additive, but rather the most common ester in wine and a natural organic compound in most fruit. Large concentrations of this substance are considered a wine fault, while barely perceptible levels contribute to complexity in the glass, and are a good thing.

152. If you taste a white wine that just seems a little past its best—perhaps low in fruit or high in alcohol, here's a trick. Pour yourself a glass of it then dribble in a little black currant liqueur known as cassis. This gives you a serving of my favorite French aperitif called Kir, pronounced "kier" as in "pier."

Part Three:

Revealing the Flavors of the World

The vine pulls elements from the soil and deposits them in the clusters of berries that swell in the sun. When you drink the wine, you drink the place. The grape grower prunes away bunches of grapes to help the plant concentrate its nutrients in a few precious bunches.

The winemaker sorts the fruit carefully, keeping only that which is good enough to eat. She presses and ferments it. Then, she matures and bottles the wine with the hope people will fall in love with it and share it with friends. Drink it at family lunches. Stash a few bottles away.

In so much of the world, the best producers are passionate artisans who care as much about the beauty of the wine as the commerce. Although this is the common denominator country to country, region to region, wine styles vary, influenced by the people and places that make them.

Bordeaux insinuates kings. Châteaux, lineage, and tradition. Prestige. Maybe that's why these wines—certainly at the top end—demand such high prices. Or maybe it's because they're so interesting; built to last, the best reds morph as they mature into allusive, sophisticated creatures bent on riveting the drinker and forcing him to take pause after each sip.

Pomerol and St. Emilion reds brim with dark chocolate, ripe cherries, and cream. Gems from places like Pauillac display open virility, with flavors of cassis and earth, spice and cigars. And the beautiful honeyed jewels from Sauternes shine golden in the glass. Like much of French living, the best of Bordeaux reminds the body of its simple lust for pleasure. And Bordeaux is just one of several superb wine regions of France. Other countries may have more wealth, power, sex appeal, sunshine, and sand, but France has its wines.

Italian wines come to life when they're uncorked, put to work at a gathering of family and friends, and surrounded by good food. They come into their own as an accompaniment. They're not solos. They are and always have been the oil that lubricates social occasions. And there's a shade and flavor to match every small patch of leathery life on the old boot of a country. Bold Barolos and Barbarescos match the hefty fare of the Northwest. The soprano Trebbianos comfortably befriend salad, fish, and oiled bread. And the sparkling Proseccos of Veneto are drank glamorously in places like Venice with small bowls of fat olives and crunchy nuts.

As well as carrying on the tradition of wine, Italy rises to the New World competition from places like California, Australia, and Chile that make fruity, friendly wine to be drank as cocktails rather than just with plates of food. Italian mavericks have stepped outside rigid wine laws to compete. Now, Supertuscans are Italy's answer to California's top Cabs, while Sicily's Merlots, Cabernet Sauvignons, and Chardonnays compete with Chile and Australia's sub-$10 wonders.

And then there is Spain. From the warm chocolate-covered strawberry and vanilla-scented wines of Rioja to the deeply misunderstood and underappreciated Sherries in the south that mix nuts and caramel, orange zest and honey in a glass and offer you a sip, Spain is about hedonism. Spanish wines pretend not to be anything but a glassful of raw gratification. And without the tradition of selling wines to cellar, Spanish bottles are cast out of the wineries aged and ready to drink.

Portugal offers light-shattered tawnies rich in roasted nut and butterscotch aromas, as well as the velvet tapestries of Vintage Port from fine years. Port is perhaps the best-known Portuguese sweetie, but Madeira is her very bewitching sister that lives on an island of the same name.

Germany gets a bad rap. Sure, the country makes sweet wines at a time when most people prefer dry but even the sweeter ones are often undervalued charms of considerable balance, harmony, and substance. Besides, so much of the world thinks dry, and drinks sweet. Perhaps the resistance to German wines, with their touch of sugar, has to do with the obstacles they can toss in the way of menu planning. Off dry ones are too sweet to pair with most main meals and too dry for desserts. The answer is in the aperitif. These wines are perfect appetite whetters. And as more people choose to drink wine as their cocktail of choice, there's no reason not to turn to Germany. Beats Coca-Cola and rum hands down.

New Zealand, Canada, California, Australia, Chile, Argentina, Hungary, and every other area under vine has a story to tell. And every wine-maker works toward the same goal of giving you and me genuine pleasure. Here's to each and every one of them.

9.

French Wine

WINES OF BORDEAUX

153. The red wines of Bordeaux are usually blends of two or more of five grapes: Cabernet Sauvignon, Merlot, Cabernet Franc, Malbec, and Petit Verdot. In Bordeaux, they blend these grapes to create power, complexity, and elegance. In France, this art of blending is called "assemblage."

154. The white wines of Bordeaux are made from Sémillon, Sauvignon Blanc, and Muscadelle.

155. Merlot is the most widely planted grape of the area and imparts rich cherry fruit and smooth freshness to wines.

156. Cabernet Sauvignon imparts high tannins and rich black currant flavors to wines, as well as aging potential.

157. In some cases, wines with high proportions of Cabernet Sauvignon made in good years by top producers can improve in bottle for more than fifty years.

158. Top Bordeaux wines are the most expensive in the world, with some bottles selling for thousands of dollars. Chateau Pétrus, widely considered the top Bordeaux wine, broke records in December 2005 when an oversized bottle of the 1982 vintage fetched nearly £19,550 (more than $34,000) at the UK auction house, Sotheby's. The oversized bottle was an imperial, which holds the equivalent to eight regular-size bottles.

159. The wines of the Médoc region of Bordeaux are ranked according to a classification drafted in 1855. The classification ranks the wines into five divisions: first growth through fifth growth. These so called cru classé wines—or classed growths—remain regarded as the top producers of the region. The only two changes since the original classification were the addition of Château Cantemerle, which was omitted by oversight and included just days after the first draft, and the elevation of Château Mouton-Rothschild in 1973 from second to first growth.

160. There are sixty-one classed growth wines in Bordeaux, based on the 1855 classification.

161. The following wines are first growths: Château Lafite-Rothschild, Château Latour, Château Margaux, Château Haut-Brion, and Château Mouton-Rothschild.

162. The following wines are second growths: Château Rausan-Ségla, Château Rauzan-Gassies, Château Léoville-Las-Cases, Château Léoville-Poyferré, Château Léoville Barton, Château Durfort-Vivens, Château Gruaud-Larose, Château Lascombes, Château Brane-Cantenac, Château Pichon-Longueville Baron, Château Pichon-Longueville-Comtesse-de-Lalande, Château Ducru-Beaucaillou, Château Cos d'Estournel, and Château Montrose.

163. Third growths include: Château Kirwan, Château d'Issan, Château Lagrange, Château Langoa-Barton, Château Giscours, Château Malescot St. Exupéry, Château Cantenac-Brown, Château Boyd-Cantenac, Château Palmer, Château La Lagune, Château Desmirail, Château Calon-Ségur, Château Ferrière, and Château Marquis d'Alesme Becker.

164. Fourth growths include: Château St. Pierre, Château Talbot, Château Branaire-Ducru, Château Duhart-Milon-Rothschild, Château Pouget, Château La Tour-Carnet, Château Lafon-Rochet, Château Beychevelle, Château Prieuré-Lichine, and Château Marquis-de-Terme.

165. Fifth growths include: Château Pontet-Canet, Château Batailley, Château Haut-Batailley, Château Haut-Bages-Libéral, Château Grand-Puy-Lacoste, Château Grand-Puy-Ducasse, Château Lynch-Bages, Château Lynch-Moussas, Château Dauzac, Château d'Armailhac, Château du Tertre, Château Pédesclaux, Château Belgrave, Château Camensac, Château Cos Labory, Château Clerc-Milon, Château Croizet-Bages, and Château Cantemerle.

166. In case you're wondering what classed growths actually taste like, here are a few of my favorites from 2001:

- Château Lynch-Bages
  Peaches and leather. Apricots and earth. Mouth-coating concentration and good structure. Flavors of black truffle, earth, sweat, and cassis. Deep brooding wine. Length: long and delicious. Zen koan in a glass.
- Château Pontet-Canet
  Black currant aromas with licorice and a slight smokiness. Balanced but firm structure and serious concentration. Palate shows flavors of warm toasted bread, licorice, and smoke. Long length. Dark, nighttime drink. Instantly gratifying.

- Château Talbot

Sour cherries and chocolate with spice and vanilla on the nose. Silky mouthfeel. Full-bodied and heavy with cherry, cassis, vanilla, and spice on the palate. Good structure, ripe tannins, balanced, concentrated, and long. Engaging.

167.

Leading Bordeaux producers get paid top-dollar for their wines. Here's a confession: I think they're often worth every cent. Here are some reasons why:

- Château Beau-Sejour Becot 2001:

Ripe on the nose with aromas of red berries, vanilla, and a powderiness somewhere. Spice. Delightful nose. Gripping tannins and ripe nuanced palate of wood, spice, vanilla, and nuts. Long. Delicious.

- Château Canon-la-Gaffeliere 2001

Slightly closed nose with earth and mineral aromas beneath cherry fruit. Palate is ripe and very compact with flavors of walnuts, tea, and cassis. Ripe tannins and good structure. Sure to develop well. Very long with a stony, detailed finish. A serious wine with a captivating style that's slightly wild.

- Château Giscours 2001

Tobacco and caramel on the nose, as well as leather and cassis. Palate is perfectly balanced with dense concentration and ripe tannins. Complex with black currant, smoke, toast, tobacco, and leather. Long length. Divine.

- Château Grand-Puy Ducasse 2001

Rich nose of ripe black currants and red forest

fruits. Balanced. Good concentration with flavors of nuts, raisins, and black currant. Complex and long.

- Château Grand Mayne 2001
  Mineral nose with cherry and vanilla. Good structure and balanced with flavors of cherry, chocolate, and vanilla. Good concentration and length.
- Château Gruaud Larose 2001
  Excellent aging potential. Ripe berry fruits on the nose with a bit of spice and a youthfulness. Ripe and full with balanced structure. Rich concentration of cassis, cherry, forest fruits, herbs, and spice. Medium to long length.
- Château Kirwan 2001
  The nose shows cassis, herbs, violet, white flowers, and roses. Structure is well-balanced. Flavors mirror the nose with a bit of spice and vanilla added. Black coffee on the finish and very long. Exquisite mix of feminine finesse and masculine muscle.

168. Many classed growth properties produce so-called "second wines," which often offer outstanding value for the money. These wines are made from slightly lesser quality or younger grapes from a celebrated property, but retain the distinct flavors of that producer and terroir.

169. Reserve de La Comtesse is the second wine of Château Pichon-Longuevillee-Comtesse de Lalande. It was first made in 1973.

170. Pavillon Rouge du Château Margaux is the second wine of Château Margaux.

171. Clos du Marquis is the second wine of Château Léoville-Las-Cases.

172. Les Carruades de Lafite is the second wine of Château Lafite.

173. Les Forts de Latour is the second wine of Château Latour.

174. The wines of the fifth growth Château Pédesclaux in Pauillac have dramatically improved recently due to many upgrades to the winery and fine-tunings of the winemaking process. Since 1996, the Jugla family, who own the Château, renovated the grape reception area of the winery, the vat-room, and the barrel cellars with the single aim of improving quality in the bottle.

175. Another much improved Bordeaux property is Château La Tour-Carnet, which was bought in 2000 by the négociant, Bernard Magrez. Under his command, and the counsel of winemaking consultant Michel Rolland, changes were introduced resulting in wines that are now fatter and richer.

176. If you like Bordeaux classed growths but don't want to pay the price, there's a bargain out there. Patrick Léon, who was the winemaker for Château Mouton-Rothschild from 1985 to 2003, bought the Bordeaux property Château les Trois Croix in 1995 where he works with his son and daughter to make outstanding wine that sells for a snip of a price of the famed first growth. I tasted the 2002 Château les Trois Croix in March 2006 and was impressed with its rich, opulent fresh berry flavors and ripe, silky tannins. It's not Mouton, but it is quite good. For a full tasting note, see the list of the best wines under $20 at the end of this book.

177. St. Emilion wines are classified differently than those from the Médoc region. According to a classification system established in 1995 and regularly amended each decade, wines are ranked into four categories— Premier Grand Cru Classé A, Premier Grand Cru Classé B, Grand Cru Classé, and Grand Cru. The reclassification of Bordeaux's St. Emilion wines will be announced in 2006, the results of which were not in when this book went to print.

178. The two Premier Grand Cru A wineries include Château Ausone and Château Cheval Blanc.

179. The eleven Premier Grand Cru B wineries include: Château Canon, Château Belair, Château Clos Fourtet, Château Trotte Vieille, Château Angélus, Château Figeac, Château Beau-Séjour Bécot, Château Cannon La Gaffelière, Château Beauséjour, Château Magdelaine, and Château Pavie.

180. A full fifty-five châteaux are ranked as Grand Cru Classé, while about six hundred châteaux fall under the grandiose sounding classification Grand Cru.

181. Pomerol is the only fine wine area of Bordeaux to never have been classified formally, but Château Pétrus and Château Le Pin are widely regarded as leading wineries in Bordeaux.

182. Since red wines from St. Emilion and Pomerol are Merlot-based, they don't age as well as those from other areas Bordeaux where the reds are made mainly from Cabernet Sauvignon. Generally, red wines from St. Emilion and Pomerol age from ten to twenty years.

183. Red wines from Pomerol tend to be heavier and richer than those from St. Emilion.

184. Bargains are available with wines from Fronsac, Bourg, and Blaye. These areas of Bordeaux offer similar Merlot-based red wines at lower prices than those from the more celebrated St. Emilion and Pomerol regions. Château les Trois Croix from Fronsac is a fine example of a good buy.

185. If you love the wines of Bordeaux so much you want to smell like them, you're in luck. Bordeaux négociant Ginestet recently released three perfumes—*Botrytis*, which smells of Sauternes with honey, candied fruit, and gingerbread; *Le Boisé* is all about oak and spice; and *Sauvignon* exudes peach and grapefruit aromas.

186. Dry white wines of Bordeaux generally come from the Graves and Entre-Deux-Mers regions. You can expect them to be crisp with restrained fruit, and a distinct mineral character.

187. Some red wines are made in Graves, but they tend to be less lush than those found elsewhere in the region despite being made from the same grapes: Merlot, Cabernet Sauvignon, and Cabernet Franc.

188. Three producers from Graves that do make very fine red wines and are in fact quite undervalued include Château des Graves, Château Olivier, and Château de Castres.

189. If you're interested in trying very good white Bordeaux from Graves, which includes the area of Pessac-Léognan, look to any of the following producers: Château Haut-Brion, Château Laville Haut-Brion, Domaine de Chevalier Blanc, and Château Pape Clément. All of these wines share pronounced minerality combined with good weight and balance beneath a sheath of fine citrus and floral flavors.

190. The area of Graves was classified in 1959 officially, ranking the best red wine and the best white wine producing properties. According to this classification, the best red wines of Graves include: Château Bouscaut, Château Haut-Bailly, Château Carbonnieux, Domaine de Chevalier, Château de Fieuzal, Château Olivier, Château Malartic Lagravière, Château La Tour-Martillac, Château Smith-Haute-Lafitte, Château Haut-Brion, Château La Mission-Haut-Brion, Château Pape-Clément, and Château Latour-Haut-Brion.

191. The best white wines of Graves officially include: Château Bouscaut, Château Carbonnieux, Domaine de Chevalier, Château Olivier, Château Malartic-Lagravière, Château La Tour-Martillac, Château Laville-Haut Brion, Château Couhins-Lurton, and Château Couhins.

192. Despite the fact that most red and white wines are made from the following eight grape varieties in Bordeaux—Cabernet Sauvignon, Merlot, Cabernet Franc, Malbec, Petit Verdot, Sémillon, Sauvignon Blanc, and Muscadelle—fourteen types of grape are actually permitted by law.

193. The regions of Barsac and Sauternes in Bordeaux are known for their sweet wines that can truly make the pulse quicken. The high humidity of these areas creates conditions that encourage a certain type of fungus called Botrytis Cinerea to attack the vines. Botrytis Cinerea, aptly called noble rot, shrivels the grapes and concentrates their sugars making sweet wine production possible.

194. In 1855, a classification ranked the top sweet wines of Sauternes and Barsac. This classification still exists to this day.

195. The best sweet wine from Bordeaux, according to the 1855 classification, is Château d'Yquem (pronounced ee-kem) from Sauternes. It is the only one adorned with the top ranking of Premier Cru Supérieur, meaning first great growth. The wines that follow its lead include:
Premier Crus (First Growths)
    Château Climens
    Château Clos Haut-Peyraguey
    Château Coutet
    Château Guiraud

Château Lafaurie-Peyraguey
Château Rabaud-Promis
Château de Rayne-Vigneau
Château Rieussec
Château Sigalas-Rabaud
Château Suduiraut
Château La Tour-Blanche

Deuxièmes Crus (Second Growths)

Château d'Arche
Château Broustet
Château Caillou
Château Doisy-Daëne
Château Doisy-Dubroca
Château Doisy-Védrines
Château Filhot
Château Lamothe-Despujols
Château Lamothe-Guignard
Château de Malle
Château de Myrat
Château Nairac
Château Romer-du-Hayot
Château Suau

196. Wondering what the fêted sweet wines of Sauternes and Barsac taste like? Here's the tasting note for the 1982 vintage of Château d'Yquem drawn up by the wine's winemaking team after tasting it on September 24, 2002: "An explosive nose that starts out with smoky, menthol, and pine aromas. The bouquet constantly evolves with a great deal of finesse, revealing overtones of candied fruit, honey, preserved orange, and vanilla. 1982 Yquem is simply marvelous on the palate. Truly great class with a fireworks display of flavors. The oak still comes through, but is well-integrated. Some spiciness on the aftertaste. Excellent balance. Huge aging potential." Voila.

197. The best sweet wines of Bordeaux are among the longest lived wines in the world. And not only do they last, but they actually improve continually in bottle for up to a century. The wines of Sauternes generally command higher prices than those from Barsac.

198. The character of a sweet wine made from grapes affected by noble rot resembles apricot in its youth, and develops into a myriad of aromas, including marmalade, peach, and honey.

199. Sauternes and fresh peaches are a royal flush in the poker game of food and wine pairing—especially when consumed with good company in the sunshine.

200. Sweet Sauternes and Barsac wines should be served chilled.

201. Looking for an alternative to Sauternes and Barsac? Similar sweet white wines from Bordeaux come from Cadillac, Loupiac, and Sainte-Croix-du-Mont, and are generally less pricey but also less intense because the growing conditions are somewhat less favorable than those of Sauternes and Barsac.

202. In 2004, the bestselling Bordeaux brand changed its blend. Mouton Cadet redesigned its labels and became fruitier to appeal to today's market. The reds are made with higher proportions of Merlot and the whites have more Sauvignon Blanc in them. Baron Philippe de Rothschild SA, which is the producer that owns the brand, sells 13 million bottles per year of Mouton Cadet in 150 countries. The range includes a red, a red reserve, a white, a white reserve, and a rosé.

203. Mouton Cadet Rouge tastes of blackberry and cherries with hints of raspberry and anise. Mouton Cadet Médoc Reserve is slightly richer and fuller and shows black pepper and vanilla flavors mingling with the red and black fruit.

204. Mouton Cadet Blanc tastes of white flowers, lime, pink grapefruit, apricot, and a hint of wet pebbles. The white reserve wine, Mouton Cadet Graves Sec, is richer and fuller. It flits from restrained lime and lemon zest, to mineral flavors edged with vanilla and smoke.

205. Mouton Cadet Rosé is a dry wine of restrained strawberry character. It's not one of the better quality pink wines out there.

206. The best value Bordeaux brand in my opinion is Calvet. The red reserve offers all the typicity of a red Bordeaux classic—cedar, pencil shavings, black currant, spice, and cherry flavors swishing around a medium-bodied wine that's always reliable, almost regardless of vintage.

207. Despite Bordeaux being quite steeped in tradition and thus rather conventional, a number of estates do practice organic viticulture. These include Château Le Puy, Château Gombaude Guillot, Château Haut Nouchet, and Domaine Ferran—not to be confused with the classed growth Le Château de Ferrand.

208. Some properties in Bordeaux have pushed past organic into controversial biodynamic methods that look to cosmic forces to help vines grow great fruit. This is somewhat surprising given the staid traditionalism of the region. Biodynamic producers include Château Falfas, Château Lagarette, Château La Grolet, Château Meylet, Domaine Rousset Peyraguey, and Château La Grave in Fronsac—not to be confused with the classed growth in Saint Emilion, Château La Grave Figeac.

209. Best recent vintages for Bordeaux's dry reds and whites include 1998, 2000, 2002, 2003, and 2005. In fact, 2005 is expected to be legendary for reds, surpassing even the superb 2000 vintage. The better wines of 2005 were not yet bottled when this book went to print.

210. Best recent vintages for the region's sweet wines include 1998, 1999, 2001, and 2003.

WINES OF BURGUNDY

211. Burgundy is made up of literally thousands of small grower-producers of varying quality, as well as large merchants called négociants. Négociants make wine from bought grapes, as well as fruit from their own vineyards.

212. Since Burgundy is so fragmented, it is one of the most confusing wine regions in the world so it's a good idea to find a knowledgeable wine merchant that specializes in the area if you're going to buy quantities of this wine. Without a doubt, it can be the most rewarding or the most disappointing purchase of wine you make.

213. The best wines of Burgundy come from leading grower-producers and négociants. Although this is fairly true of most places in the wine world, it's especially true in Burgundy.

214. Reputable négociants in Burgundy include: Joseph Drouhin, Faiveley, Louis Jadot, and Bouchard Père et Fils. They each make a wide range of wines with magnetic value for the money.

215. The appellation controllée system of France regulates the provenance of the wine, not the quality of it. Nowhere is this small fact more important than in Burgundy, where great vignerons toil beside very average ones. This means the producer is more important than the vineyard location when buying Burgundy.

216. Four grapes go into Burgundian wine: Chardonnay and Aligoté are the white ones and Pinot Noir and Gamay are the reds. The best quality white wine is made from Chardonnay while Aligoté grapes make a cheap and cheerful wine for quaffing. For reds, the top-dollar stuff comes from Pinot Noir and the less expensive, easy drinking wine is made from Gamay.

217. The subregions of Burgundy from north to south are Chablis, the Côte d'Or (made up of the Côte de Nuits and the Côte de Beaune), the Côte Chalonnaise, Mâconnais, and Beaujolais. Each region produces different styles of wine.

218. In Burgundy, vines are matched to soil type. Chardonnay thrives on limestone-based soils, while Pinot Noir plantings do well on marl- and clay-based plots. Gamay is planted on the granite soils of southern Beaujolais.

219. In the northern Burgundian region of Chablis, wine-producing areas are ranked from best to average, with the main classifications of Grand Cru, Premier Cru, Chablis, and Petit Chablis.

220. In Chablis, seven plots of land are considered Grand Cru. These include: Les Clos, Vaudésir, Balmur, Blanchot, Preuses, Grenouilles, and Bougros. Bottles from these areas will carry the phrase Grand Cru as well as the name of the demarcated regions. Grand Cru vineyards can produce the most polished and ageworthy wines in all of Chablis when made by the right vigneron. Grand Cru Chablis is at best a dignified wine with considerable depth of character.

221. Forty plots of land are designated Premier Cru Chablis, the best known of which include: Les Fourchaumes, Les Montmains, Les Beauroy, Les Vaudevey, and Les Vaillons. Wine from these areas will note the words, Premier Cru Chablis, and the region it's from on the label. The best Premier Cru Chablis represents heroic control showing all the subtly, grace, and understated power of a tightly bound orchestra.

222. Wines simply labeled Chablis are from the classic heart of the region notwithstanding the celebrated Premier and Grand Cru plots of land. This wine can be quite good but it is made to drink young—within a few years of vintage.

223. Wines labeled Petit Chablis are made from grapes grown on lesser quality soils outside the traditional heartland of the Chablis region. This wine can be quite good but often lacks the more pronounced mineral character of that labeled Chablis.

224. Jean-Marc Brocard is an impressive Chablis producer keen to retain the very mineral flavors that are the traditional hallmark of the region's wines despite the fashion for fruitier versions. If you like classic Chablis, hunt down wines by this honorable producer.

225. Jean-Marc Brocard produces a range of majestic Chablis wines with characteristic aromas of dry stones, lemon zest, steel, and sometimes grapefruit. They're usually quite crisp, quenching, and long. Of particular interest is Brocard's Premier Cru range aptly named Mineral, Extreme, and Sensuel.

226. If you love Chablis and are looking for a consistent, affordable bottle, look to those by the cooperative, La Chablisienne. Their wines range from Grand Cru to Petit Chablis and are classic-tasting, consistently good quality, and relatively low priced. Also, given La Chablisienne is responsible for about one quarter of all Chablis produced, the bottles are fairly easy to find.

227. In Chablis, the soil is limestone with a top layer of Kimmeridgian clay—a type of marl high in marine fossils. This clay imparts a distinctive flavor of wet stones to the wines. For this reason, Chablis is a wine that can easily taste of its place, which is why it is a shame to make wines that are so fruit-laden that they blur the beautiful but subtle reflection of this fine terroir.

228. Chablis can be immeasurably elegant and satisfying but it is an understated wine easily overpowered by strong foods. My favorite food and wine pairing right now is hot, buttered lobster with Chablis from Les Clos.

229. The most revered wines of Burgundy come from the Côte d'Or. And wines from this region have earned this stature through hundreds of years of demonstrating greatness.

230. The best red Burgundy comes from quality producers in the Côte de Nuits, while the best white comes from leading producers in the Côte de Beaune—together, these regions make up the Côte d'Or.

231. Red Burgundy from the Côte de Nuits represents the Holy Grail toward which so many other Pinot Noir producing regions in the world aspire. No one has matched it yet. But there are good ones being produced in patches in the U.S. and New Zealand. Red Burgundy can be brilliant stuff, which is why it fetches very high prices.

232. The official hierarchy of wine in the Côte d'Or region of Burgundy is as follows: Grand Cru, Premier Cru, village wines, regional wines.

233. The following vineyards of the Côte d'Or have Grand Cru status:
Mazis-Chambertin
Ruchottes-Chambertin
Chambertin Clos-de-Bèze
Chapelle-Chambertin
Griotte-Chambertin
Charmes-Chambertin
Le Chambertin
Latricières-Chambertin
Clos de a Roche
Clos St-Denis
Clos des Lambrays
Clos de Tart
Bonnes Mares
Le Musigny
Clos de Vougeot
Grands Échezeaux
Échezeaux
Richebourg
Romanée-St-Vivant
Romanée-Conti
La Romanée
La Grande Rue
La Tâche
Le Corton
Corton-Charlemagne
Chevalier-Montrachet
Bienvenues-Bâtard-Montrachet

Le Montrachet
Bâtard-Montrachet
Criots-Bâtard-Montrachet

234. You can identify a Grand Cru wine by the fact the vineyard name stands alone on the label. Grand Cru wine accounts for less than 2 percent of the wine produced in Burgundy.

235. There are 561 Premier Cru vineyards in Burgundy, accounting for 11 percent of the wine produced in the region. These wines are recognizable because the commune and vineyard name will generally both appear on the label. Such as: "Nuits-St.-Georges 1er Cru," followed by "Les St. Georges."

236. If a wine names a district or commune on the label, such as Mâcon or Volnay, the wine will have been made from fruit grown in that particular place and is a so-called "village wine."

237. If the word Bourgogne is on a wine label, such as Bourgogne Aligoté, it is a regional wine, meaning it can be produced from fruit grown anywhere in Burgundy.

238. Good value can be found with both village and regional wines from quality producers, but these wines are not made for aging.

239. Louis Jadot's Côte de Beaune-Villages 2000 is an example of the fine quality négociants can deliver. This Pinot Noir is packed with black cherry, ripe raspberries, and blueberries, as well as hints of roasted meat and earth. At under $20, it's perfect for those who want an introduction to red Burgundy.

240. Pommard—not to be confused with the Champagne house, Pommery—is an area of the Côte de Beaune that makes red wines from Pinot Noir.

241. Domaine Prince Florent de Merode shows how seductive Pinot Noir from Pommard can be with its Clos de la Platière 2003 wine. The nose of black truffle, earth, and smoked meat leads to a palate of mushroom, truffle, game, plum, and cranberry. I could drink lashings of this wine with roasted turkey.

242. Puligny-Montrachet is an area in the Côte d'Or that can produce white wines of cut-crystal elegance.

243. Domaine Olivier Leflaive's 2002 Puligny-Montrachet is an excellent version of top-notch white Burgundy from the Côte d'Or. Roasting hazelnuts, tranquil vanilla, lemon zest, warm caramel, butter pastry, and on and on. It's an inspired wine that will last until about 2009.

244. Two more very good white Burgundies are Maison Champy's St. Romain 2000—think freshly baked orange pound cake: all butter, orange zest, and toasty caramelized edges—and Domaine Larue's 2002 Les Cortons, St. Auben 1er Cru, which tastes of buttered pecans mixed with candied orange and lemon.

245. A red Burgundy well worth the price of less than $25 is Prince Florent de Merode Ladoix "Les Chaillots" 2003. This glossy wine is everything a good quality Pinot Noir from Burgundy should be—elegant, complex, and supremely capable of maturing gracefully. Les Chaillots resonates with aromas and flavors of game, mushroom, truffle, mixed forest fruits, smoke, and spice. It drinks well now, but will last another five to ten years. This wine is from Ladoix in the Côte de Beaune.

246. Domaine Georges Mugneret produces consistently excellent red wines from Nuits St. Georges. They will set you back about $50 but they are reliable dinner party or special occasion wines that deliver clean, juicy, complex sips every time.

247. Domaine J. Confuron Coteditot in the Côte d'Or produces top quality red wines that are ripe and rich in fruit and fairly full-bodied for Pinot Noir. These wines are undervalued today because they haven't attained quite the following in North America that can push up the price into the stratosphere…yet. The Premier and Grand Cru wines by this producer can mature for more than a decade in good years.

248. Young red Burgundy from the Côte d'Or tastes notoriously of tinned strawberries and ripe raspberries. The best, well-aged ones are silk-robed blessings that resound with flavor after flavor—game, earth, cherry, raspberry liqueur, truffles, beef, pepper, toast, mushrooms, vanilla, mocha, chocolate, stones, and on and on. But remember, the Pinot Noir grape is not generally dense in color and concentration like the wines of Bordeaux or the Northern Rhône. They are stylistically very different.

249. Reliable producers of red Burgundy from the Côte d'Or include Domaine Thierry Mortet, Domaine J. Confuron Coteditot, Domaine J. Chauvenet, Domaine Leroy, Nicholas Potel, Domaine Méo-Camuzet, Château de Chorey, Joseph Drouhin, Faiveley, Bouchard Père et Fils, Domaine Georges Mugneret, Domaine Leflaive, and Domaine Olivier Leflaive.

250. White wines from the Meursault area of the Côte de Beaune taste quite rich and butterscotchy, and are particularly popular in North America. Due to the demand, the prices can be steep so it's worth knowing wines from Rully taste similar and often sell for much less. One such bottle is Joseph Drouhin's 2003 Rully 1er Cru from the Côte Chalonnaise, which tends to retail for under $20. This wine offers a classic flurry of lemon, cream, vanilla, nuts, and toffee.

251. Wines from the Côte Chalonnaise taste similar to those from the Côte d'Or but are a little simpler and usually made to drink young. The four main winegrowing areas are Rully, Mercurey, Givery, and Montagny. Red wines labeled with these names are made from Pinot Noir while the whites from these areas are made from Chardonnay.

252. For good wines from the Côte Chalonnaise, look to those by Faiveley, François Lumpp, and Henri & Paul Jacquesson.

253. A wine labeled Bourgogne Côte Chalonnaise can be made from Pinot Noir or Chardonnay grapes grown anywhere in the Côte Chalonnaise area.

254. Wines labeled Mâconnais are from the area of the same name between the Côte Chalonnaise and Beaujolais in Burgundy. The wines can be white or red. If it's white, it will be Chardonnay, and if it is red it can be made from either Gamay or Pinot Noir.

255. White wines labeled Mâcon or Mâcon-Supérieur can be pretty good value and will generally taste of melon and buttered toast.

256. Red wines called Mâcon or Mâcon-Supérieur are usually made from Gamay and are average at best. Choose Bourgogne Rouge instead because it's usually a much better value for about the same price.

257. Wines labeled Mâcon-Villages or Mâcon followed by a village name are a cut above those labeled simply Mâcon or Mâcon-Supérieur. Since they come from the southern reaches of the region, more sunshine means riper and richer wines.

258. Wines labeled Saint Véran, Pouilly-Loché, Pouilly-Vinzelles, or Pouilly-Fuissé are some of the best wines of the Mâconnais region. These wines are always white and made from Chardonnay grapes.

259. Pouilly-Fuissé is quite a popular wine, particularly in North America, and the prices are somewhat inflated so it's best to choose wines from Saint Véran, Pouilly-Loché, Pouilly-Vinzelles instead, which are similar. Pouilly-Fuissé is not to be confused with Pouilly-Fumé, the white wine produced in the Loire made from Sauvignon Blanc grapes.

260. Gamay grapes make Beaujolais. This simple child of a wine is quick, eager to please, and born in the southernmost region of Burgundy. Beaujolais is best drank before it's two years old and tastes like a mouthful of ripe mixed berries—fairly tart, ready to drink, and low in tannin. It's a light style of red wine that is very food friendly because it can be paired with a broad range of dishes.

261. Beaujolais is low in tannin because it's made by carbonic maceration. Without getting technical, carbonic maceration simply means the grapes aren't crushed before they're fermented. While Beaujolais is made partially this way and partially by the traditional method of crushing grapes before fermenting them, which imparts some tannin from the skins, Beaujolais Nouveau is made entirely by carbonic maceration, creating a wine that is both uncoarse and unsubtle. A juicy style of easy-drinking wine.

262. Carbonic maceration can impart aromas of banana and bubblegum to a wine.

263. Beaujolais Nouveau is released on the third Thursday in November after the vintage and cannot be sold by merchants or growers after the following August 31st. About a third of all Beaujolais is sold as Beaujolais Nouveau.

264. Many producers in Beaujolais are going out of business due to low sales. This is a shame given how delicious and versatile this wine can be.

265. Beaujolais is an excellent wine to serve at a wedding. It is easy to drink, easy to like, goes well with food, and it's not very expensive.

266. Expect to hear more about Beaujolais in the near future. To combat low sales, Beaujolais launched a $5 million marketing campaign in 2005 to raise awareness of its wines in the U.S. The campaign runs until 2008.

267. Georges-Deboeuf and Louis Jadot are two reliable producers of Beaujolais.

268. Burgundy produces less than half the amount of wine as Bordeaux. Plus, cheap and cheerful Beaujolais accounts for about half of all Burgundy wine produced. This means there's relatively little high quality Burgundy to feed the huge demand for this wine, so prices can be very high. Top-quality Burgundy sells for hundreds of dollars per bottle.

269. Faiveley sculpts a drink that clearly expresses the clean raspberry character of ripe Pinot Noir. It's called La Framboisière and it is from the Mercurey area in the Côte Challonaise.

270. The one place in Burgundy that produces Sauvignon Blanc is Saint Bris in Yonne.

271. If you see Irancy on a label, it's made from Pinot Noir. It's either rosé or red wine and, if it's red, it will generally be lighter and more sour than other Pinot Noir-based red Burgundies.

272. Both red and white top-quality Burgundy wines are usually aged in oak. The casks are often old wood as to not overpower the delicacy of the wines with oak flavors, but new oak barrels are sometimes used for the richer wines.

273. The nearby forests of Vosges, Nevers, and Allier provide much of the wood for the barrels of Burgundy.

274. If you see the phrase "Bourgogne Passetoutgrains" on the label, the wine is a blend of Pinot Noir and Gamay.

275. As one of the oldest wine regions in the world with vineyards dating back to the Roman times, soil erosion and years of pesticide use in Burgundy have been a problem. For this reason, some producers are turning to organic methods to help heal the soil and regain its vitality. The most extreme form of organic farming is called biodynamic viticulture; as well as minimizing pesticides, herbicides, and fungicides, this method looks to the cosmos to infuse the vines and land with spiritual energy.

276. Domaine Michel Lafarge, Domaine Leroy, Domaine D'Auvenay, Domaine Giboulot, Domaine Leflaive, Domaine Pierre Morey, Domaine Trapet Pere et Fils, Domaine du Comte Armand, Domaine Montchovet, and Domaine des Vignes du Maynes are all biodynamic producers in Burgundy. They are also organic given biodynamic is an extended version of this method of production.

277. Best recent vintages for white Burgundy include 1999, 2000, 2001, and 2002.

278. Best recent vintages for red Burgundy, not including Beaujolais, are 1999, 2001, 2002, and 2003.

279. Best recent vintages for Beaujolais were 2000 and 2003 but, with this wine, always reach for a bottle from the most recent year.

WINES OF CHAMPAGNE

280. Champagne is identifiable blind by the scent of toast, cooked apple, and butter pastry and a restrained, elegant palate with zippy acidity. The true form is inimitable.

281. Champagne can only be produced within a specific region of France called Champagne, centered on the towns of Reims and Epernay.

282. Champagne is made from one or more of three grape varieties: Pinot Noir, Pinot Meunier, and Chardonnay. Pinot Noir gives body and power to the wine, Pinot Meunier imparts suppleness and fruitiness, and Chardonnay lends finesse and delicacy.

283. Although Pinot Noir and Pinot Meunier are red grape varieties, the grapes are pressed gently enough to keep the skins from imparting color to the wine. In the case of pink Champagne, some color is intentionally bled from the red grape skins.

284. The two ways of making pink Champagne are the traditional *saignée* method and by blending red and white wines. The *saignée* method involves making a rosé wine by allowing brief contact between the pressed grape juice and the red grape skins.

285. Pink Champagne is becoming more popular in almost every major market. From 2004 to 2005, sales of the pink fizz rose 23 percent in the UK, 40 percent in the U.S., 50 percent in Spain, 20 percent in Belgium, 10 percent in Italy, and 78 percent in Australia.

286. A blanc de blancs Champagne is made from 100 percent white grapes (Chardonnay) while a blanc de noirs is made exclusively from red grapes (Pinot Noir and Pinot Meunier). Red grapes are often called black grapes in the wine trade—hence the name blanc de noirs, which is of course French for *white of blacks*.

287. Ever wonder how they get those bubbles in the bottle? Champagne houses make still wines first, called vins clairs, from each grape variety and plot of land. Then they blend them to achieve an intended style. After bottling this still wine, yeast and sugar are added to start a second fermentation. The yeast consumes the sugar, produces alcohol and carbon dioxide in the sealed bottles, and creates bubbly wine. After this second fermentation, the wine is matured at least fifteen months with the spent yeast to impart characteristic flavors and aromas. The bottles are slowly turned upside down to encourage the yeast to collect in the bottleneck, where it is removed before the bottles are topped up with wine, recorked, wire muzzled, and foil wrapped.

288. The large foil wrap around the neck of a Champagne bottle was used traditionally to hide the gap between the cork and the wine because bottles were not always topped up.

289. Champagne without bubbles is also produced in the region under the name Coteaux Champenois. This name applies to all red, white, and pink still wines from the area. These wines are fairly rare and tend to be tart and thin.

290. Mousse is the French term for Champagne's bubbliness.

291. You probably know that James Bond's favorite fizz was Bollinger, but did you know Winston Churchill's favorite tipple was Pol Roger Champagne? Sir Winston Churchill said, "I cannot live without Champagne. In victory, I deserve it, and in defeat, I need it!"

292. The reason Pol Roger was Winston Churchill's favorite tipple was because he had a close relationship with Odette Pol Roger, a director of the famous Champagne house. The two were introduced at a lunch in 1944 at the British Embassy in Paris. According to the house of Pol Roger, Odette had served as a courier for the French Resistance during the years of occupation and Churchill was charmed by her spirit. Churchill's relationship with Odette led to him naming one of his racehorses "Pol Roger."

293. When Winston Churchill died in 1965, the Pol Roger family paid tribute to him by placing a black band of mourning on all of their Champagne bottles destined for the UK for a period of twenty-five years.

294. How do you know if a bottle of Champagne is dry or sweet? Generally, if a label has the word *brut* on it the Champagne will taste dry. Bottles labeled *extra sec* or *sec* are actually off-dry, while those labeled with *demi-sec* are sweet. Doux Champagne is quite sweet, but not cloying because Champagne always has enough acidity to preserve that feeling of freshness on the palate.

295. By law, the word Champagne must be written on the part of the cork that will actually be in the bottleneck.

296. Champagne corks look like giant mushrooms when they're extracted from the bottles but in fact, they're cylinder-shaped when they're put in. They return to their original shape when soaked in water.

297. Champagne must be aged for at least three years before it is released for sale. Better houses exceed this legal limit.

298. Every year, Champagne houses release nonvintage Champagnes, which are blends of wines from two or more years. Each brand of Champagne makes its own house style, which is consistent year to year in its non-vintage bottlings. Knowing these house styles can help you choose a style that suits your taste.

299. Krug Champagne's majestic nonvintage, called Grande Cuvée, is very full-bodied with flavors of caramelized nuts, cooked apple, and buttered toast. It is very much like a bubbly white Burgundy. The intense flavors result from the fact Krug makes all its Champagne in small oak casks, and is the only house that does so.

300. The house of Louis Roederer, which makes the coveted prestige cuvée Cristal, also makes the more affordable non-vintage Champagne Brut Premier. This wine is excellent quality at a fraction of the price of Cristal, and can be aged for several years after purchase to increase the wine's complexity. Its style is lighter-bodied and elegant, with flavors of cooked apple and pastry, much like tart tatin.

301. Bollinger is a muscular style of Champagne often described as quite masculine—not surprising it was chosen to be the favorite of the screen hero Mr. Bond. Its nonvintage version is powerful and bold for a bubbly because of its high proportion of Pinot Noir in the blend. It also tends to express biscuity flavors, ripe yellow apple, hints of buttered caramel, and often cherry and coffee. Quite stylish.

302. Pol Roger Brut Reserve, this house's nonvintage wine, is characterized by a fresh bread nose and a lean palate of apples, milk chocolate, and toast.

303. Jacquesson's nonvintage, called Cuvée No 729, is all nuts and cream, recalling cashews and apples with hints of toast.

304. The nonvintage by Deutz is called Brut Classic and is rich and complex with flavors of biscuit, honey, toast, and apple.

305. Vintage Champagne is a blend of wines made from grapes of a single year. It is up to individual Champagne houses to declare a vintage year—meaning, make vintage-dated wines—and the better houses only do so in the very best years.

306. Most Champagne houses produce a prestige cuvée, which is the top-of-the-line wine from the house. The house of Pol Roger makes Cuvée Sir Winston Churchill, Louis Roederer makes Cristal, Moët & Chandon makes Dom Pérignon, and Taittinger's makes Comtes de Champagne, to give you a few examples. These wines are made from the best quality fruit, and are richer, more complex, and more ageworthy than other wines of the house.

307. Pol Roger's grand cuvée—Cuvée Sir Winston Churchill—was named to salute the historic hero himself. Churchill liked robust, full-bodied Champagne, and this wine is dominated by Pinot Noir to pay tribute to his tastes. The very first Cuvée Sir Winston Churchill was launched in 1984, from the classic 1975 vintage—ten years after his death. Since the inaugural vintage, it has only been made in the best years.

308. Louis Roederer's grand cuvée—Cristal—was made at the request of the Tsar Alexander II, who ruled Russia in the late nineteenth and early twentieth centuries. The Tsar was a wine connoisseur who made it his mission to acquire the very best wines for himself. On one occasion in 1876, the Tsar pointed out to his sommelier that there was no visible difference between his Champagne and that which his guests could purchase themselves so he asked the house of Louis Roederer to provide his personal cuvée in a crystal bottle. In response to his request, Louis Roederer made Cristal specifically for him and bottled it in crystal. Louis Roederer Cristal is no longer bottled in crystal of course.

309. Louis Roederer Cristal is the only Champagne to have a flat-bottomed bottle, which the Tsar Alexander II insisted on to avoid assassination attempts being made by hiding explosives in the punt.

310. In 1909, Tsar Nicholas II ordained the house of Louis Roederer to be the official supplier to the Imperial Court of Russia. Louis Roederer Cristal first became available for general consumption in 1924 for Europe and after World War II for other countries. It is now one of the most sought after wines of celebrities and wine connoisseurs alike.

311. Louis Roederer and Pol Roger are two of the few remaining family-owned houses of considerable size in Champagne. Roederer has been owned by the same family since 1776 and Pol Roger since 1849.

312. Many top Champagne houses are controlled by the luxury goods conglomerate Louis Vuitton Moët Hennessy, including Moët et Chandon, Dom Pérignon, Krug, Ruinart, Mercier, and Veuve Clicquot. These wines are consistently good quality but expensive.

313. Lower priced Champagne can be found but many are dire. How do you save money on Champagne without compromising taste? Look for the letters "RM" on a label, which stands for "récoltant-manipulant," which is basically French for grower-maker. These Champagnes are made by small family-owned outfits that grow their own grapes and stake their businesses and reputations on making very good quality wines. They tend to be lower priced because they don't have the same caché as the bigger houses.

314. Champagne—especially nonvintage—should be chilled well before serving. Doing so not only ensures an ideal drinking temperature, but also subdues the pressure in the bottle so it can be opened safely.

315. To open a bottle of Champagne, point it away from you and others. Carefully unwrap the foil and muzzle while keeping your hand over the cork. Grip the cork tightly and turn the bottle, gently easing the cork upwards and out. Contrary to popular belief, there should be no loud popping sound.

316. Flutes are the most appropriate glasses for Champagne rather than the traditional saucer-like "coupe," which encourages the wine to go flat and warm quickly.

317. A flute glass should be not be filled more than 1/2 to 2/3 full. This level gives the aromas room to vaporize in the glass.

318. Choose flutes without intentional scratches on the bottom. These scratches make larger, less appealing bubbles than those that form naturally in glasses without these marks.

319. The Champagne houses of Fleury, David Léclapart, and Bedel all practice biodynamic viticulture.

320. Reliable big producers of bubbly include Louis Roederer, Ruinart, Pommery, Pol Roger, Bollinger, Krug, Billecart-Salmon, Jacquesson, and Taittinger.

321. Reliable smaller houses include Selosse, Larmandier-Bernier, Egly-Ouriet, and Lilbert.

322. Best recent vintages for Champagne were 1996, 1999, 2002, and 2004. The 2005 vintage is expected to be outstanding.

WINES OF ALSACE

323. Alsace grows mainly German grape varieties but, due to the climate and French winemaking tradition, the wines are richer and drier than those of Germany.

324. The grapes of Alsace are Riesling, Sylvaner, Gewurztraminer, Pinot Blanc, Pinot Gris, Pinot Noir, Muscat, and Chasselas.

325. Alsacean white wines often share a subtle smoky aroma and an air of utter conviction about the grape variety they articulate.

326. New oak is rarely used in Alsace because the purity of fruit flavor is the goal of the region's winemaking.

327. Alsacean producers often label their wines with the grape variety from which they're made. If a grape appears on a label of an Alsacean wine, you can be sure the wine is made from 100 percent of that grape variety. This is not the case with many other growing regions.

328. About a quarter of all Alsacean wine is Riesling. And an Alsacean Riesling tastes vivacious and steely, ages well, and can be dry or sweet.

329. A producer of particularly fine Riesling is Domaines Schlumberger. Its Les Princes Abbes Riesling is extraordinary. Aromas of lime and butterscotch lead to a palate of lime, butter, minerals, and a lovely orange zest character. Beautiful stuff. Dry, crisp, but with excellent concentration, body, and length. Worth every penny and a bargain at about $15.

330. If this book had a section for best wines under $25, Domaines Schlumberger's Riesling Saering 2004 would lead the list. It's class in a glass. Basil, pepper, restrained apple, oregano, smoke, white flowers, rhubarb, lime, and the list goes on. Complex, well-toned, long, and capable of maturing admirably.

331. Vignobles Charles Koehly makes Riesling sing with the St. Hippolyte 2002 version that exudes flinty aromas from the first whiff, then moves toward fresh lemons and limes before mellowing back into flinty notes and citrus zest. This wine is bracingly crisp with a long finish, balanced structure, and a high thrill factor.

332. Gewurztraminer from Alsace is spelled without the "umlaut" accent—that double dot over the u used in the German spelling. Since Gewurztraminer grapes are pink skinned, the wine can be quite coppery colored in the glass. And Alsacean Gewurztraminer is generally full-bodied, high in alcohol, low in acidity, and tastes of lychees and roses.

333. The masterful vigneron Léon Béyer is known for his outstanding Gewurztraminer wine in Alsace. Look for his name on bottles.

334. Pinot Blanc is a very light, fruity wine that is best drank young. It is the type of wine one would order by the *pichet* in a Paris café to have with a casual lunch.

335. Pinot Gris, also called Tokay-Pinot Gris, smells and tastes of spiced peaches. It is full-bodied, rich, and in best cases can age up to fifty years. It is my favorite variety from Alsace right now.

336. Domaine du Bollenberg produces outstanding Tokay Pinot Gris. The 2001 shows peach and spice on the nose, followed by flavors of full ripe peach with nutmeg, cinnamon, and pepper.

337. Tokay-Pinot Gris dry white wine has a full-bodied, almost oily mouthfeel with good acidity and excellent balance. It's long, tightly wound, and drinking well now, but will last several more years.

338. Pinot Noir from Alsace produces either light red or a deep rosé wines. To my mind, the best Pinot Noir still comes from Burgundy.

339. Alsacean Muscat and Chasselas are minor grape varieties from Alsace, accounting for about 4 percent of the plantings. Muscat tastes quite grapey and makes a good aperitif while Chasselas makes a very light, fruity table wine.

340. Domaine Marcel Deiss produces an excellent Muscat d'Alsace that offers a mouthful of pure fruit with good length.

341. Alsace can produce excellent sparkling wine under the name of Crémant d'Alsace, which is fruity, refreshing, and a brilliant outside-in-the-sun aperitif or cocktail alternative. Dopff au Moulin's Cuvée Julien Brut shows lots of ripe yellow stone fruit with a squeeze of lemon, followed by a long, dewy lemon-orange finish.

342. Two outstanding producers in Alsace, whose wines are worth scouting out, are Josmeyer and Domaine Zind-Humbrecht.

343. Olivier Humbrecht, the winemaker at Domaine Zind-Humbrecht, makes stellar wines. The wine simply called Zind is a very affordable example of what this wine master can do with grapes. This is interesting, delicious, age-worthy stuff—white pepper and peach nose followed by a rich, spiced peach palate with refreshing acidity, full body, dense fruit, and a bone dry finish. Good length, too.

344. Josmeyer's 2002 Riesling "LeKottabe" is underpriced at about $20. This wine is built to last and offers a nose of wet pebbles leading to a juicy lemon-lime character on the palate, with a bright seam of acidity. Excellent fruit expression, lean, and long.

345. Although Trimbach is one of the best-known Alsacean producers, I find only their higher end stuff to be good value for the money.

346. Trimbach's celebrated Clos Ste-Hune wine is a revered stunner. It's a Riesling of great grace, concentration, and longevity that tastes of ripe limes, warm clay, roasted spices, smoke, fresh bread, and on and on. It has earned quite a following and, perhaps as a result, a bottle will set you back more than $100.

347. If a wine from Alsace is labeled Vendange Tardive, it means the wine is a "late harvest" style and full-bodied. Unlike late harvest wines from North America or Germany, Vendange Tardive wines from Alsace are not always sweet; they can be dry, off-dry, or medium sweet as well.

348. Domaines Schlumberger's Vendange Tardive Cuvée.Christine 2000 Gewurztraminer is a medium sweet version that is sumptuous with classic lychee flavors resounding with orange zest, rose petals, and hints of roasted nuts.

349. Sélection de Grain Nobles on a label means the wine is sweet and the grapes from which it was made were affected by noble rot, imparting a honey and marmalade character on the nose and palate.

350. Grand Cru wines from Alsace indicate they're made from grapes from a top quality growing region and low yielding vines. Fifty vineyards in the region have this status, but the classification is just a few decades old and controversial. I would suggest buying your Alsace wines based on the producer's reputation rather than Grand Cru status.

351. Here's a list of biodynamic producers in Alsace, all of which produce very good wines:
Domaine Pierre Frick
Domaine Marcel Deiss
Domaine Zind-Humbrecht
Domaine Martin Schaetzel
Domaine Marc Tempé
Domaine Ostertag
Domaine Kreydenweiss
Domaine Josmeyer
Domaine Valentin Zusslin

352. Today, more than thirty wine properties in Alsace are organic or biodynamic.

353. The best recent vintages for Alsace are 2000, 2002, and 2003.

WINES OF THE LOIRE

354. If you like crisp white wines and refreshing light reds with restrained fruit, the Loire is the region for you. These wines are like a quick dip in the lake on a hot day.

355. The white grapes of the region include Muscadet, Chenin Blanc, Chasselas, and Sauvignon Blanc. The red grapes of the Loire are Cabernet Franc (also called Breton), Cabernet Sauvignon, Gamay, Cot (also called Auxerrois or Malbec), Groslot (also called Grolleau), and Pinot Noir.

356. Muscadet is the most well-known wine from the Loire and tends to taste of lemon with hints of green apple. It's always dry and sour, and should be drank young—ideally within a year or so of the vintage.

357. Seafood is the classic match to Muscadet because the two don't overpower each other.

358. Muscadet is always a light- to medium-bodied wine. By law, the alcoholic strength can never exceed 12 percent.

359. If the label reads Muscadet Sur Lie, the wine has been bottled without removing the lees—or spent yeast—from the cask or tank. As a result, the wine retains a yeasty character reminiscent of warm bread and may have a few gentle bubbles from a slight spontaneous refermentation in bottle. *Lie* is the French word for lees.

360. Gildas Cormerais Muscadet de Sèvre et Maine 2004 Sur Lie is fresh and reminiscent of a thick layer of tart lemon curd on a slice of freshly baked bread.

361. Chenin Blanc wines from the Loire can be dry, sweet, sparkling, or still. Regardless of style, the wine always has a streak of bright acidity.

362. Very well-made wines from Chenin Blanc age beautifully. The Savennieres Roche aux Moines 1999 by Château de Chamboreau in the Loire Valley is a fine example. It's a complex, elegant wine that's still quite youthful despite some years of bottle age. Lovely honeyed apricot aromas lead to a surprisingly dry palate with clean white flowers, vanilla, almond, incense, and peach flavors that linger.

363. The Loire also produces Vouvray, a white wine made from Chenin Blanc that can range from dry to sweet.

364. An example of a dry Vouvray that's richer and fleshier than most is Domaine du Viking's 2001. This wine shows honey, melon, green apple, flowers, and tufts of green grass with interesting mushroom aromas and good length.

365. Sweet Vouvray is made in good years only when noble rot affects the grapes. Noble rot shrivels the grapes, concentrating the sugars and imparting honeyed flavors to wine.

366. Vouvray always strikes the palate with quite a bit of zeal. It has high acidity so even when the wines are sweet, they have a refreshing, palate-cleansing quality.

367. Domaine Nicolas Gaudry makes good quality Chasselas, a white wine that's crisp and dry with sprightly peach and green apple fruit.

368. Cabernet Franc and Gamay are the two main red grapes of the Loire and create wine that is relatively thin and sour—best for early drinking. Don't age this wine.

369. Sauvignon Blanc from the Loire is often grassy and mineral tasting, quite unlike the gooseberry juice of the New World.

370. The famous Sancerre wine comes from the Loire. It's usually white and made from Sauvignon Blanc, though is sometimes red and made from Pinot Noir. You'll pay a premium for the Sancerre name.

371. A reliable producer of Sancerre is Château de Tracy, whose wines tend to be very lean and stony tasting with a splash of sourness to freshen the mouth after each sip. These wines will usually keep for up to about five years from the vintage date and a bottle will cost you about $25.

372. White Sancerre is almost always fermented in stainless steel, giving the fruit a clean flavor. Having said that, some are successfully fermented in wood, creating complex nutty, spicy, or vanilla-like flavors depending on the wood used.

373. Pouilly-Fumé—not to be confused with Pouilly Fuissé from Burgundy— is also made from Sauvignon Blanc. Both Pouilly-Fume and Sancerre show a distinctly mineral character due to the soil where the grapes are grown. This stony flavor is usually described as flinty or reminiscent of gun smoke.

374. Like Sancerre, you'll pay a premium for the Pouilly-Fumé name, but it can be a very satisfying tipple.

375. The three rosé wines from the Loire are Rosé d'Anjou, Rosé de Loire, and Cabernet d'Anjou.

376. Rosé d'Anjou is often slightly sweet and blended from Grolleau, Cabernet Franc, and Gamay grapes. It's the lowest quality of the three pink wines of the region. Grolleau is a traditional red grape of the Loire that's being phased out gradually and replaced by Cabernet Franc and Gamay.

377. Rosé de Loire is always dry and must include at least 30 percent Cabernet Franc or Cabernet Sauvignon in the blend. This wine is invariably better than Rosé d'Anjou.

378. The best of the three pink wines of the Loire is Cabernet d'Anjou, which must be a blend of Cabernet Franc and Cabernet Sauvignon grapes. It is usually medium sweet.

379. A wine by the name Saumur-Champigny from the Loire is a red from Cabernet Franc with flavors of red berries and grass.

380. Domaine du Ruault Saumur-Champigny 2003 is a cracking example of this lovely bistro wine style. It's a charming traditional raspberry-and cherry-infused wine with that hint of herbaceousness that makes it a fine food partner. Drink it young.

381. Chinon—not to be confused with the white grape Chenin Blanc—is one of the best red wines of the Loire. It is made from Cabernet Franc, and is light and fruity with an underlying minerality. Domaine Bernard Baudry is a good quality producer of Chinon.

382. Bourgueil and St-Nicolas-de Bourgueil are both red wines made from Cabernet Franc. Much like Chinon, these pale reds are crisp with restrained mixed-berry flavors and hints of grass.

383. Ferme de la Sansonnière, Domaine des Maisons Brulées, Château Tour Grise, Clos de la Coulée de Serrant, Domaine de l'Ecu, Domaine Saint Nicolas, Domaine Pierre Breton, Domaine des Sablonnettes, Domaine Mosse, and Olivier Cousin are all biodynamic producers in the Loire.

384. Best recent vintages in the Loire for red wines are 2000, 2001, 2003, and 2004.

385. Best recent vintages for the Loire's whites are 1999, 2000, and 2004.

WINES OF THE RHÔNE

386. The wines of the northern Rhône tend to be full-flavored, tannic Syrah-based wines, and big, white, fleshy peach-pear wines from the Viognier grape. Some whites are also made from the apricot-scented Roussanne and pineapple-marzipan flavored Marsanne grapes.

387. The red wines of the southern Rhône are made from a blend of up to thirteen grape varieties, the most important of which are Grenache, Cinsault, and Mourvèdre. The whites are made from Roussanne, Clairette, Ugni Blanc, and seven other lesser varieties.

388. The northern Rhône produces the most serious wines of the region and accounts for just 5 percent of all wine produced in the whole Rhône region. The eight wine-producing areas of the north include Côte Rôtie, Condrieu, Château Grillet, St. Joseph, Hermitage, Crozes-Hermitage, Cornas, and St. Peray.

389. The red wines from Côte Rôtie, St. Joseph, Hermitage, Crozes-Hermitage, and Cornas are generally 100 percent Syrah, although producers are allowed by law to add certain white grapes. The dominant flavors are blackberry, black pepper, dark chocolate, and smoke.

390. Côte Rôtie literally means roasted slope. This small area in the Rhône receives extra helpings of sunshine as the name implies and, as a result, produces a ripe style of muscular red wine that lasts for decades. Because the area is small, both the wines and the prices are legendary.

391. Guigal is a top producer of Côte Rôtie, as well as wines from the entire Rhône region. Wines from the hand and heart of this exceptional vigneron, Marcel Guigal, deliver good value from the simple Côtes-du-Rhône to the very exciting single domaine wines that are dignified expressions of glory. Guigal's 2003 Côte Rôtie La Landonne is a big, bold, turbulent wine of intense complexity, showing wave after wave of black cherries, licorice, coffee, chocolate, pepper, smoke, pebbles, and earth flavors. In the glass, this wine flits from joy to joy once it has had time to bloom in bottle. It will last for forty years or so.

392. Condrieu is another small wine region in the northern Rhône. It is revered for its white wine made solely from the Viognier grape. The wine, at best, is as fleshy, sensual, and satiating as any wine has a right to be. La Doriane by Guigal is my favorite Condrieu; it's gorgeous with tightly bound fruit wrapped around a firm mineral core. At about $75 per bottle, it is an indulgence. But it's worth every penny with its unctuous peach and apricot flavors, full-body, and reverberating finish. I particularly love it with a fettuccine Alfredo, pan-fried chicken, and fresh herbs.

393. Château Grillet is a very small white wine appellation in the northern Rhône that makes a wine by the same name. It, like Condrieu, is made from 100 percent Viognier, but because the grapes tend to be picked earlier in Château Grillet than in Condrieu, the wine is more austere, tart, and lean. Generally, Condrieu delivers better value than Château Grillet, although the latter wine can generally age longer.

394. St. Joseph is a region producing wine of variable quality. The appellation expanded from a tight 360 hectares in the late 1980s to more than 800 hectares today. This sprawl means a lot of young vines and lesser quality terrain are in the mix, given the best fruit comes from older vines and the most suitable vineyard conditions. When buying wine from St. Joseph, buy from a reliable producer.

395. The red wines of St. Joseph are made from Syrah and the whites are made from Marsanne and Rousanne grapes. Two reliable producers of wines from St. Joseph are Domaine Jean-Louis Chave and M. Chapoutier.

396. Hermitage makes robust and majestic red wine that ages well. It is made from 100 percent Syrah, and has serious aging potential. One of the best producers of Hermitage is Domaine Jean-Louis Chave. Curiously, but not surprisingly, red wines of Hermitage had such status in the eighteenth and nineteenth centuries that its wines commanded prices similar to those of Bordeaux-classed growths.

397. Hermitage is also home to white wine that is almost as exciting as the red, yet not as well-known, made from Marsanne and Rousanne. This wine is medium- to full-bodied and dry, and accounts for about a third of the wine of the appellation.

398. Crozes-Hermitage is the area surrounding Hermitage, which makes less intense red wine with short-term aging potential. It produces about eight times the amount of wine as the revered Hermitage.

399. While red Hermitage is 100 percent Syrah, red Crozes-Hermitage can range from 85–100 percent because producers are legally allowed to add up to 15 percent white grapes to soften the wine. White wines from the area are a blend of Marsanne and Rousanne grapes.

400. The white wines of St. Joseph, Hermitage, and Crozes-Hermitage can be lovely—clean, lively, and fresh—but they don't age well.

401. The cooperative Cave de Tain produces beautiful wines from Hermitage and Crozes-Hermitage. Particularly interesting are the white Crozes-Hermitage if you can find them. I remember first tasting these wonders when visiting the area in 1999 and thinking they resembled the creamy vanilla and slightly caramelized flavors of rich crème brullée, along with refreshing apricot and floral notes. Excellent quality and balance at affordable prices—especially when purchased at the cooperative itself.

402. Wines from Cornas are meaty, mighty Syrah-based reds with good aging potential. Cornas wines rival those of Hermitage. Auguste Clape is the leading producer and his wines are generous offerings of rich, ripe berry fruit with a characteristic smoky, savory quality.

403. St. Péray produces white still and sparkling wines from Marsanne and Roussanne grapes. Cave de Tain's Saint Péray is a playful fawn of wine with aromas of delicate white flowers, bright citrus zest, white peach, and vanilla.

404. Red wines from the northern Rhône are smoother than ever before because many producers are destemming the grapes before pressing them and replacing older barrels with new oak.

405. Wines from the southern Rhône are mainly red and generally blended wines with a high proportion of fruity Grenache seasoned with other grapes, including Carignan, Cinsault, Mourvèdre, and Syrah. These wines contrast sharply with the single-variety Syrah heavyweights of the northern Rhône.

406. You know a wine is from the southern Rhône when any of the following names appear on the label: Côtes du Rhône, Côtes du Rhône-Villages, Côtes du Rhône-Villages with a village name appended (such as Rasteau), Châteauneuf-du-Pape, Gigondas, Lirac, Tavel, or Vacqueyras.

407. Perrin & Fils wine from Rasteau is consistently appealing. The 2003 vintage will cellar nicely for a good six to eight years from vintage and harbors considerable depth of character. The wine tastes of ripe raspberries and blueberries dipped in dark chocolate, with hints of vanilla and spice on the finish. Wines like this, which sell for under $20, are why the wines from this region have gained a following. Perrin & Fils vineyards are now undergoing organic certification.

408. Château de Beaucastel, a renowned estate in Châteauneuf-du-Pape, was officially certified organic in 2000. This producer is admired for its consistent quality. Its top wines are simply labeled Château de Beaucastel and tend to be big extravagant offerings of black and ripe red fruit, smoky meat, pepper, spice, mineral, and herbs.

409. Coudoulet de Beaucastel is the second wine of Château de Beaucastel. It doesn't have quite the same depth as the wine simply called Château de Beaucastel, but is lush with lots of spicy, meaty, fleshy fruit. It's the kind of mouthful of joy that justifies the popularity of Rhône reds.

410. Wines labeled Perrin & Fils are made by the same man who makes Château de Beaucastel wines—Pierre Perrin.

411. Red wines from Châteauneuf-du-Pape usually exude tobacco aromas. They give the impression of a quiet, generous old Frenchman, with a cigarette dangling from his mouth.

412. If you're looking for great red wine similar to Châteauneuf-du-Pape but more reasonably priced, try a bottle from Gigondas in the southern Rhône. This wine tends to be more tannic than Châteauneuf-du-Pape but it becomes quite friendly with bottle age. Typical Gigondas wine shows lots of black stone fruit, leather, and spice, and should age five years or so from the vintage date before you try them.

413. All M. Chapoutier wines have Braille labels due to a friendship between winemaker Michel Chapoutier and the blind soul and jazz musician, Ray Charles.

414. Tavel is a rosé from southern Rhône made from Grenache and Cinsault grapes. It is always bone dry and usually rather high in alcohol. Many French feel this is their country's best pink wine. It can be quite good, but must be consumed very young and well chilled.

415. Beaumes-de-Venise is a fortified sweet wine, known as a vin doux naturel, from the Rhône Valley. Made from the Muscat grape, a glass of Beaumes-de-Venise makes a sprightly aperitif or dessert wine. It's also quite reasonably priced compared to the sweet wines from Barsac and Sauternes, but don't expect the same richness and concentration.

416. The list of biodynamic producers in the Rhône is long. It includes Domaine Les Aphillantes, Domaine Pierre André, Domaine de Villeneuve, Montirius, Domaine Viret, and the mighty Maison Chapoutier.

417. Organic producers include those biodynamic vignerons named above as well as Clos du Joncuas, Perrin & Fils, Château de Beaucastel, and Guigal.

418. The Rhône Valley has had a number of excellent vintages recently with 1998, 1999, 2000, 2001, 2003, and 2004 being the best years.

WINES OF PROVENCE AND CORSICA

419. Provence makes some of the best rosé wines in France—fresh, ripe, delicious quaffers that taste of mixed berries, peach, white flowers, and often spice. They're based on Cinsault and Grenache grapes, and should always be consumed chilled and young, within about year of the vintage. To me, rosé from Provence captures the essence of southern France.

420. If you think pink from Provence means sweet, think again. The region is responding to a global demand for drier rosés.

421. Reliable producers of Provence rosé include Domaine Rabiega, Domaine Sorin Roland Bouchacourt, Domaine St. André de Figuière, Château Margillière, and Château de Fonscolombe.

422. Provence also makes some very good quality red and white wines. Domaine Richeaume and Domaine St. André de Figuière are two of the better producers of red and white wines from Provence.

423. Wines labeled Côtes de Provence can have up to thirteen grape varieties in the blend, including: Carignan, Cinsault, Grenache, Ugni Blanc, Clairette, Mourvèdre, Rolle, and Sémillon.

424. Red wine accounts for just 15 percent of production in Provence, but a growing number of producers are trying to make seriously high-quality reds, particularly in the area called Bandol. Bandol in Provence makes powerful, spicy red wines from Mourvèdre grapes, which imparts rich flavors of leather and black pepper, as well as a typical gaminess.

425. Perhaps the most notorious producer in Bandol for quality reds is Domaine Tempier. The wines from this estate are big and bold with amplified flavors reminiscent of sweaty saddle leather, rich ripe blueberries, spice, earth, and caramelized meat drippings—not for the faint of heart. Domaine Tempier also makes a rosé that is rich in color, berry fruit, and spice.

426. A lesser-known producer of very good red Bandol is Domaines Bunan. The producer's flagship wine is Château de la Rouvière, with tastes of roasted meat, smoky blueberries, cassis, and spice. It sells for about $30.

427. Bandol rosés are made from Mourvèdre grapes, showing an unmistakable and charming spiciness. The pinks from Château de Pibarnon are reliably good.

428. Corsica is an island in the Mediterranean under French jurisdiction that produces red, white, and rosé wine. The wine is quite average generally, and is not widely exported.

429. If you see a wine named, "Vin de Pays de l'Île de Beauté," it's from Corsica.

430. Domaine Pero Longo is a biodynamic wine producer in Corsica. Château de Roquefort, Château Romanin, and Domaine Hauvette are three biodynamic producers in Provence.

431. Domaine de Trevallon, Château Sainte-Anne, and Château Margillière farm organically.

432. The 2000 and 2001 vintages were very good in both Provence and Corsica.

WINES OF SOUTHWEST FRANCE

433. If you like Sauternes but balk at the price tag, the Montbazillac area of Southwest France offers a very similar but less expensive alternative. A reliable producer from here is Château les Sablines.

434. If you like fine Bordeaux red wine, consider the wines from Bergerac, Côtes de Duras, Buzet, and Côtes du Marmandais. These are Bordeaux look-alikes made from the same grape varieties as their more famous cousin—Cabernet Sauvignon, Merlot, Cabernet Franc, Petit Verdot, and Malbec—at a fraction of the price.

435. Cahors is a region in Southwest France known for its muscular reds. One good example is the wine aptly called Pur Plaisir, by Château Haut Monplaisir. The 2001 vintage is an intense offering of smoked meat, the forested great outdoors, and lots of rich black stone fruit. Beautifully untamed and rugged to the core.

436. The main grape of Cahors is Auxerrois, also called Cot in the Loire and Malbec in Argentina. These wines generally exude aromas of blackberries, black plum, and dried fruit. Wine from this variety in France is generally more tannic than the slightly rounder and softer version from Argentina.

437. A leading estate in Cahors is Clos Triguedina. The Auxerrois-based wine, called Prince Probas, is a heavyweight that needs several years in the cellar before uncorking. The 1999 reveals rich fruit, chewy tannins, and layers of coffee, spice, plum, and cassis.

438. Domaine Le Bouscas and Domaine de Souch are two biodynamic producers from Southwest France.

439. Southwestern France enjoyed a streak of excellent vintages from 1998 to 2001.

WINES OF LANGUEDOC AND ROUSSILLON

440. The Languedoc still suffers from a grim reputation as a producer of large amounts of poor wine, which was indeed the case until fairly recently. Today, excellent wines are starting to be made by some quality-minded producers investing heavily in the region. Producers to watch for include Château de Caraguilhes from the area of Corbières, Château Laville-Bertrou from Minervois, and Château Pech Redon from Faugères.

441. The better quality reds of the region are made from Cabernet Sauvignon, Merlot, Syrah, and Mourvèdre, while the best whites come from Chardonnay, Sauvignon Blanc, and Viognier. Usually, grape names appear on labels of wines from this region to compete with New World producers having success with the same strategy.

442. One of the biggest secrets of the Languedoc is Limoux's sparkling wine, called Blanquette de Limoux. Blanquette de Limoux is made mainly from the Mauzac grape, which tastes of apple skins, along with 10 percent Chardonnay and Chenin Blanc for a bit of complexity and elegance. With the delicacy of Champagne at a fraction of the price, it's worth tasting. Look to the reputable producer, Chandenier.

443. Crémant de Limoux is another appealing sparkling wine from the area. It differs from Blanquette de Limoux by having a larger proportion of Chardonnay and Chenin Blanc—up to 30 percent instead of 10 percent.

444. Sparkling wine from Limoux predates that of Champagne by more than a century.

445. Generally, like the Languedoc, the Roussillon region makes quite average wines but some very good producers exist, such as Domaine Gauby and Clos des Fées.

446. About 80 percent of France's Vin Doux Naturel, a fortified sweet wine, comes from the Roussillon. These wines are usually are made from Grenache and Muscat grapes and are at least 14 percent alcohol.

447. Vin Doux Naturel can be a delicious and inexpensive dessert wine. It's made in the same way as Port—stopping the fermentation process before all the grape sugar has been converted to alcohol by killing the yeast by adding grape spirit.

448. Red Vin Doux Natural from the Banyuls and Maury regions of the Roussillon is made from black Grenache grapes, and can be an inexpensive alternative to ruby Port.

449. Domaine du Traginer, Domaine Beau-thorey, Domaine Gauby, Domaine de Fontedicto, Le Petit Domaine de Gimios, Clos du Rouge Gorge, and Domaine Cazes are all biodynamic producers in this region.

450. Domaine Léon Barral is an organic wine producer in the Languedoc-Roussillon.

451. Languedoc-Roussillon enjoyed very good vintages in 2000 and 2001.

VIN DE PAYS

452. Vin de Pays is a classification that was established in France in the 1970s. It came into effect to upgrade the quality of wines from parts of the south of France.

453. Vin de Pays is generally better quality than Vin de Table. Grapes for Vin de Pays must be from specific regions of France—instead of from anywhere in the country for Vin de Table.

454. Grapevines for Vin de Pays must meet yield restrictions, whereas vines for Vin de Table aren't restricted this way. Lower yields mean more concentrated fruit, which is a contributing factor to making good wine.

455. Although a step up from Vin de Table, Vin de Pays wines are made under less stringent quality control restrictions than those designated as AOC, which stands for Appellation d'Origine Contrôlée. That doesn't necessarily mean that Vin de Pays is inferior to AOC wine, but this is usually the case.

456. Domaine Laurent Miquel shows what can be produced under the Vin de Pays banner with the stunning wine, Nord-Sud Viognier. This wine from the Languedoc shows floral and nutty flavors surrounding a rich core of succulent peaches and pears.

457. Levin Sauvignon Blanc 2004 Vin de Pays du Jardin de la France is another lovely expression of the Vin de Pays category. This wine is a refreshing, zippy version of the grape with tart gooseberry and hints of both green asparagus and crushed stones. Jardin de la France means it's from the Loire.

WINES OF THE REST OF FRANCE

458. Bouzy Rouge is no joke. It is a still wine from Pinot Noir that comes from the region called Bouzy, which is in the Champagne region of France.

459. Vin Jaune is an unfortified Sherry-like wine that's delicate and nutty, full-bodied and dry. It's made in eastern France, in an area called Jura.

460. Vin de Paille, also made in Jura, is a lusciously sweet dessert wine that can keep for decades in bottle—unopened, of course. Unlike Sauternes, which is made from grapes shriveled by noble rot, grapes destined for Vin de Paille are dried on straw in winery attics over the winter to concentrate the sugar before pressing and fermenting.

461. Vineyards even exist in Paris. The most famous one is Clos Montmartre, just steps from Sacré Coeur and the Moulin Rouge.

462. Domaine Prieuré Saint Christophe is a biodynamic producer in Savoie.

463. Domaine André et Mireille Tissot is an organic producer in the Jura region.

10.

Italian Wine

WINES OF NORTHWEST ITALY

464. Piedmont is arguably the most important wine region of Northwest Italy, making the famous Barolo and Barbaresco wines. Barolo and Barbaresco come from regions of the same names. Both are challenging, heavy wines made from the Nebbiolo grape.

465. Barolo is a deep, resolute expression of Nebbiolo heaving with aromas and flavors of roses, tar, and licorice, as well as black and red stone fruit. The wine is always rich in tannins and acidity, as well as alcohol and fruit extract. It is a wine that comes into its own after many years of bottle age.

466. Enzo Boglietti produces exemplary Barolos brimming with ripe plum, tobacco, chocolate, smoke, and all that's fine in the world. Dip in after you've patiently granted the bottles some years to rest. Another noteworthy producer is Cavallotto, that makes chocolatety, spicy, fruit-drenched Barolos. Good winter wines.

467. Traditional Barolos are best ten to twenty years after the vintage. They tend to be unpleasant and tough before then.

468. Barbaresco is a strapping wine of considerable vigor, but less intense than Barolo. Another point of difference is Barbaresco matures quicker than Barolo, coming into its own five to ten years after vintage.

469. Some producers are making softer, easier drinking Barolos and Barbarsecos in response to the global demand for fruitier wine that's ready to drink young. Ceretto is a producer making Barolo wines in this more accessible style and Angelo Gaja makes a modern and friendly style of Barbaresco.

470. The hallmark flavors and aromas of Barbaresco wine are pretty much always tar and roses.

471. Ada Nada is a reliable producer of traditional Barbarescos that taste of spice, tar, roses, and often hints of espresso.

472. Bruno Rocca makes Barbarescos with reams of hefty black pepper and black forest fruits, as well as stones, leather, tar, and the usual perfume of roses.

473. Barolo and Barbaresco were sweet wines until the mid to late nineteenth century. Today, they are all dry, massive reds.

474. The area of Trentino in Northwest Italy makes a wine called Teroldego Rotaliano, named for the Teroldego grape from which the wine is made. These wines are deeply colored with black and red berry flavor and the unmistakable hint of tar. These wines are low in tannin but high in extract and acid, so expect lots of sour fruit. They are also slightly bitter on the finish, which is the inherent wine style rather than a flaw. These wines should be drank within about five years of the vintage.

475. Concilio makes a very good Teroldego Rotaliano with all the charm and elegance of a gracious Old World wine as well as the easy accessibility of a fruity New World one.

476. About half of the wine produced in Piedmont is Barbera, which are often labeled Barbera del Piemonte, Barbera d'Alba, or Barbera d'Asti. It is a full-bodied, ruby-colored wine with high acidity made from a grape of the same name. It is the people's wine—an inexpensive, easy-to-drink food wine.

477. Think of Barbera as the quintessential Italian mother—generous, reliable, and almost indispensable to family meals. Barbera is relied on by the people of Northwest Italy to go with their traditional fare of antipasto, risotto, meat, cheese, pasta, and pesto. It is probably the best value red wine you can buy from Italy.

478. In 1982, Giacomo Bologna made a Barbera called Bricco dell'Uccellone. This wine was different than any other Barbera because it came from carefully managed vines with reduced fruit yields, and was fermented in new French oak barrels—a technique not traditionally applied to Barbera winemaking. The low yields made riper, more concentrated Barbera while the new oak barrels changed the structure and flavor substantially; oak-fermented Barbera is softer and spicier. This new approach caught on and other Barbera producers are quickly following suit.

479. Today, there are traditional and modern Barbera's available. The way to tell the difference is to know the producer—again a reason to search out a knowledgeable wine merchant.

480. Castello Calosso is a name to watch for when shopping for Barbera d'Asti. Recently, ten top wine producers of the Asti region collaborated to try to produce what they would deem the best Barbera in the world. They grow their own fruit and vinify it in their own wineries, but they all subscribe to a shared set of standards and use the same label design.

481. Dolcetto is a native red grape of Northwest Italy that produces fruity, affable wine of the same name. Dolcetto is dry, low in tannin and acid, and tastes of fresh mixed berries and almonds. Best drank young—meaning within a year or two of the vintage noted on the bottle—it is great midweek quaffer to pair with almost anything.

482. Look for Dolcetto d'Asti by Corino. This producer makes wines of consistently good quality with clean, ripe black cherry, blackberry, and raspberry fruit; hints of violet; and a kick of spice.

483. The Moscato grape makes a sparkling wine called Moscato d'Asti, which works well as an aperitif or refreshing accompaniment to a dessert of fresh pineapple. It's delicate, light-bodied, medium-sweet, and low in alcohol.

484. La Spinetta makes a lovely Moscato d'Asti called Vigneto Biancospino. Threaded through with lacy acidity, this fresh fruity sparkler is the perfect al fresco aperitif.

485. Gavi is a still white wine from Cortese grapes. It is dry and lean with zippy acidity, and mineral and lime flavors.

486. A good producer of Gavi is Castello Di Tassarollo. Here, all grapes are hand-picked before being pressed and made into wine. About 10 percent of the wine is aged briefly in barrels to add a bit more character to the Cortese grape. The wines tend to taste of citrus, green apple, almonds, and a hint of anise.

487. A biodynamic producer in the Piedmont region of Northwest Italy is Cascina Degli Ulivi.

488. Two organic producers in Northwest Italy are Cascina La Pertica and Tenute Loacker.

489. Years 2001 and 2004 were the best recent vintages in Northwest Italy.

WINES OF NORTHEAST ITALY

490. Northeast Italy makes Valpolicella, Soave, Amarone, Prosecco, and the varietally labeled wines from the usual international grapes—Cabernet Sauvignon, Chardonnay, Merlot, Sauvignon Blanc, and so forth.

491. Valpolicella is a light red, refreshing wine best drank young. The grapes used to make Valpolicella are Corvina, Rondinella, and Molinara, and the resulting wine tastes of cherry and red plum.

492. Is it possible for a wine to smell and taste of a place? Yes. Bertani's Villa Novare Valpolicella Classico 2004 takes me to Italy in a sip. Earth, black plum, and mixed ripe forest fruit. Outstanding value.

493. Masi is another reliable producer of Valpolicella. Its Bonacosta Valpolicella Classico, easily identifiable by the plain black bottle that simply reads Masi Valpolicella with a vintage date, is all fresh, clean cherries and plums. It is medium-bodied and as easy to match with food as France's Beaujolais.

494. If a wine is called Valpolicella Superiore it must be aged for at least a year before bottling, and it must be at least 12 percent alcohol.

495. Recioto della Valpolicella is made from semidried grapes and the wine is sweet. It is also fuller-bodied than an ordinary Valpolicella.

496. If you see the word "ripasso" on a bottle of Valpolicella, it had the unpressed skins of Amarone wines added during winemaking to add extra flavor and alcohol. A wine marked "ripasso" is more voluptuous than an ordinary Valpolicella.

497. Valpantena's Falasco Valpolicella Ripasso 2003 is an excellent example of the richness the ripasso process can impart to wine. This wine starts with cigar shop aromas and leads to a ripe, full palate of chocolate-covered black and red cherries. Delicious.

498. Soave is a delicate white wine tasting faintly of apples and almonds. It is made near the city of Verona from the grapes Garganega, Trebbiano di Soave, Trebbiano Toscano, Chardonnay, and Pinot Bianco. It's widely exported and often inexpensive. Look for good producers—such as Coffele, Pieropan, and Bertani, as well as Inama—that make particularly fine versions of this wine.

499. Roberto Anselmi, a small but leading producer in Veneto, switched from calling his wine Soave DOC to Veneto IGT in 2000 because he felt the laws governing the Soave DOC production encouraged thin, poor quality wines. His white wine, Capital Foscarino, is stellar. Made from low yielding Garganega and Trebbiano grapes, the 2004 vintage starts with a nose of ripe red cherries and red licorice—you would be forgiven for thinking this wine was red if tasted blind—then takes the palate by storm with fresh lemon, mineral, and ripe apple. It's a long, rigorous version of this classic grape blend. Fabulous.

500. Amarone is a deep, rich, evocative red wine that often reaches 15 percent alcohol by volume. Although it is made from the same grapes as Valpolicella—Corvina, Rondinella, and Molinara—the grapes destined for Amarone are dried before pressing, concentrating the wine.

501. Reliable producers of Amarone are Tenuta Sant'Antonio, Allegrini, and Manara.

502. In the difficult 2002 vintage, Masi didn't make its coveted Amarone wines. Instead, the fruit went into Masi's Supervenetian wine, Campofiorin, which sells for about a quarter of the price of this producer's Amarones. As a result, the 2002 Campofiorin offers outstanding value for the money. It's quite rich and velvety, and dirt cheap for what's in the bottle. It sells for less than $15.

503. Prosecco comes from the Veneto region, and is a pear-flavored bubbly. Prosecco is made from the indigenous grape of the same name.

504. Bisol makes first-rate Prosecco. The Bisol Prosecco di Valdobbiadene Crede is particularly delicious with flavors of pear and citrus.

505. In Venice, bartenders mix Prosecco with fresh white peach juice to make a cocktail called a Bellini. The drink was invented at Harry's Bar in Venice in the 1940s, named after the fifteenth-century Venetian painter Giovanni Bellini.

506. Prosecco and Bellinis are drank as aperitifs in Venice with finger foods called Cicchetti. Cicchetti can range from small pieces of meat or fish to wee rice balls stuffed with olives and are served at the bar. Cicchetti is eaten standing up with drinks.

507. In 1969, Italy gave Prosecco its own controlled appellation, which is called DOC Prosecco di Conegliano-Valdobbiadene. Valdobbiadene and Conegliano are geographic areas where Prosecco has been grown historically. Until the early part of the twentieth century, Prosecco was mainly a still wine.

508. Prosecco is now bubbly because it's better that way. The high acidity, light body, and aromatic character work well with fizz, making it a great refresher.

509. Many varietal labeled wines come from the Friuli region. One of the area's top winemakers is Silvio Jermann. He makes very good Pinot Grigio that's riper and more interesting than most. His so-called Jermann Pinot Grigio 2004 is a full, fleshy expression of peach and sage with hints of roasted nuts. Drink all Pinot Grigio young.

510. Pinot Grigio is the same grape as Pinot Gris from Alsace but they taste very different. In Italy, the grapes are harvested less ripe, creating a lighter, leaner, and much more neutral tasting wine reminiscent of flowers and lemons. Pinot Gris tastes of spiced peach.

511. Radikon is a biodynamic producer in the Friuli-Venezia region of Italy.

512. The best recent vintages for North-east Italy were 1997, 1998, 2000, 2003, and 2004. In 2002, the area suffered a terrible hail-storm; it was not a good year for wine.

WINES OF TUSCANY

513. In Italy, wines are labeled DOCG, DOC, IGT, or VDT (Vino da Tavola/table wine). In theory, these are descending quality levels with the most restrictions applied to DOCG winemaking and fewest to Vino da Tavola. However, an increasing number of respected Italian winemakers—particularly in Tuscany—avoid government regulations by making top-quality wine but labeling it IGT or Vino da Tavola.

514. Supertuscan wines are an interesting recent phenomenon. In the 1970s, some modern-thinking winemakers in Tuscany began making wines using grape varieties and methods that didn't meet the DOCG or DOC requirements. They labeled them table wine (VDT). Despite this traditionally lower classification, these wines took the world by storm, stirring enthusiasm that exists to this day, and fetching high prices.

515. Supertuscan wines are usually blends of French and Italian grape varieties, particularly Cabernet Sauvignon and Sangiovese. They are also frequently matured in small oak barrels to create more complexity.

516. Though you will never see the word Supertuscan on a label, wines known to be of this genre include Sassicaia, Tignanello, Siepi, Vigna d'Alceo, and Masseto.

517. I was blown away the first time I tasted Tignanello, which was at La Famiglia restaurant in London. This wine is a rich, smooth, mouth-coating elixir of black cherry, vanilla, chocolate, and earth. Delicious with a plate of angel hair pasta, Parmesan Reggiano, and freshly grated white truffle. Yum.

518. Chianti is a region in Tuscany that makes a wine by the same name. It's always made from Sangiovese grapes and tastes of cherries. A wine labeled Chianti Classico means the wine comes from grapes grown in the original center of the Chianti region, recognized for having the best soils for growing Sangiovese.

519. In 1716, the Grand Duke of Tuscany issued an edict officially recognizing the boundaries of the Chianti district. This proclamation was the world's first legal document defining a wine production zone. Chianti Classico is therefore the world's first ever legally demarcated wine region and the original boundaries remain today.

520. Chianti Classico's wines are identifiable by an image of a Black Rooster on the bottle. The Black Rooster guarantees the wine's authenticity and verifies that it has passed strict quality controls.

521. Chianti Classico's black rooster symbol dates back to the Middle Ages. Legend has it that the behavior of a black rooster decided the zone's political fate. The Chianti territory fell between to the two medieval republics of Florence and Sienna. Both places wanted control of the region so it became a theater of almost continuous clashes. Tiring of the turf wars, the two cities agreed to define their boundaries via an unusual contest between two horsemen, one from each city. The frontiers would be drawn at the point where the riders met after setting out at cockcrow from their respective cities. Each city selected a rooster as their "starter pistol." Sienna selected a pampered white rooster plump from its rich diet and used to the usual dawn crowing; Florence chose a black rooster that was fed very little and kept in darkness so it was unaware of sunrise or sunset. On the appointed day, the black rooster awoke long before dawn with a rumbling stomach to crow for its breakfast. As a result the Florentine rider set off early and met the Sienna horseman at Fonterutoli, just a few miles from Sienna, thereby earning the largest share of the Chianti Classico region for Florence.

522. The unique terroir of Chianti Classico gives the wine a distinct violet aroma. The violet characteristic is found most prominently in the more premium Chianti Classico Riservas such as those from Vicchiomaggio, Fontodi, Barone Ricasoli, or Castello di Fonterutoli.

523. Chianti Classico from Castellare di Castellina, Marchesi Antinori, Castello di Ama, and Castello di Fonterutoli all represent very good value.

524. Castellare di Castellina Chianti Classico 2003 is pure violets and anise on the nose, leading to a charming and seductive mix of roasted tobacco, cherry, almond, violets, and aniseed on the palate.

525. Chianti Rufina can be the finest Chianti you can buy when made by a quality producer. Rufina is a Northeastern area in the Chianti region where the soil and climatic conditions are extraordinary.

526. Frescobaldi produces an outstanding Chianti Rufina called Nipozzano Riserva. It's rich, concentrated, and benefits from a few years of bottle age as well as double decanting.

527. Since 2000, Chianti producers have been allowed by law to add up to 20 percent of less traditional grape varieties, including Cabernet Sauvignon, Merlot, or Syrah. This revision is changing the traditional flavor of Chianti.

528. Wines named Brunello di Montalcino are powerful expressions of the Sangiovese grape; they are the Barolos of Tuscany. Brunello is the name for the local strain of Sangiovese that makes deep, seamless, powerful wines with significant tannin and length. Brunello di Montalcino must be 100 percent Brunello.

529. Castello Banfi is a reliable producer of very good Brunello di Montalcino. The 1999 wine is complex, with flavors of chocolate, anise, leather, and rich black forest fruits.

530. Castello Banfi is a leader in controlling the winemaking process from vineyard to bottle, and the quality of this producer's wines is outstanding. The prices are still fairly affordable, too.

531. Vino Nobile di Montepulciano is made from another local strain of Sangiovese called Prugnolo Gentile. Often blended with other grapes, Vino Nobile di Montepulciano is lighter and offers less aging potential than Brunello di Montalcino. A reliable producer of Vino Nobile di Montepulciano is Poliziano.

532. Carmignano is a small area west of Florence that has been revered for its fine red wines since the Middle Ages, and is now home to DOCG wines. If you see the word Carmignano on the label, know it's a blend of Cabernet Sauvignon and Sangiovese, and sometimes Canaiolo.

533. If you visit Tuscany, you will probably be offered Vin Santo as a dessert wine. Vin Santo is a wine with varying levels of sweetness. The local custom is to have it in a small tumbler with dry biscotti for dunking—a potent and delicious way to end a meal.

534. Although usually sweet, Vin Santo can be bone dry and resemble Fino Sherry. This drier style is best drank as an aperitif.

535. Vin Santo is made by pressing semi-dried grapes, then sealing the pressed juice in small casks with yeast leftover from the previous batch. The wine is left to ferment slowly for up to six years, taking on nutty and caramelized flavors. Essentially, this process deliberately oxidizes the wine, giving it a Sherry-like character and a lovely amber color. Vin Santo is made from the local white grapes Trebbiano and Malvasia.

Vin Santo should not be confused with Vino Santo, a sweet wine from Trentino in Northwest Italy without the oxidized, Sherry-like nuance.

536. Organic producers in Tuscany include Buondonno, Poggio Trevvalle, Casina di Cornia, Tenuta di Valgiano, and Massa Vecchia.

537. Biodynamic producers in Tuscany include Colle Massari, Castello dei Rampolla, Stella di Campalto, Fattoria Castellina, Caiarossa, and Fattoria Cerreto Libri.

538. Best recent vintages in Tuscany were 2001, 2003, and 2004.

WINES OF THE REST OF CENTRAL ITALY

539. Verdicchio is a dry white wine that comes from the Marche region in central Italy. It's a dry, crisp, restrained wine with bitter almonds on the finish. It's best drank within a year of the vintage date.

540. A reliable producer of Verdicchio is Fazi-Battaglia, which is a négociant that controls more than 20 percent of production of this white Italian wine.

541. Marche is on the eastern seaboard of Italy, where the locals consume fresh fish and seafood with lashings of Verdicchio.

542. Marche also produces some good red wine, a fine example of which is the Velenosi "Il Brecciarolo" Rosso Piceno Superiore 2002 made from Sangiovese and Montepulciano grapes. Smooth cherry, cinnamon, and sandalwood flavors swirl around in this easy-to-like wine.

543. Orvieto is a white wine from the Umbria region of Central Italy. It is generally a dry, medium- to full-bodied wine that's slightly lemony and made from Trebbiano, blended with Malvasia, Verdello, Grechetto, and Drupeggio. Bigi is a reliable producer.

544. Lungarotti is a leading producer from Umbria famous for its excellent red wine, Rubesco Reserva. It's made mainly from Sangiovese grapes and tastes of ripe red berries and spice, with long, lingering length.

545. The two main wines from the Abruzzo region are Montepulciano d'Abruzzo and Trebbiano d'Abruzzo.

546. Montepulciano d'Abruzzo is a red wine made from the Montepulciano grape, and is round, deeply colored, and easy to drink. It's best drank young—within a few years of vintage—and it tastes of plum, blackberries, and sweet cherries. This is a wine that generally delivers quite good value for the money.

547. Not to be confused with Vino Nobile di Montepulciano, Montepulciano d'Abruzzo is made from an entirely different grape—one called Montepulciano rather than Prugnolo Gentile. The wines are smooth with flavors of plum and cherry.

548. Trebbiano d'Abruzzo is a white wine from Abruzzo made from the lemony Trebbiano grape. The wine is crisp and fairly neutral with hints of lemon zest and nuts. Drink it young and chilled.

549. A reliable producer of Montepulciano d'Abruzzo and Trebbiano d'Abruzzo is Masciarelli.

550. You might be starting to realize another secret of Italian wine: the names are usually based on the grape variety, place of origin, or both, so if you're intrigued by the country's wine, familiarizing yourself with some of the local grapes and the country's geography is an excellent way to get to know Italian wines.

551. Emidio Pepe Abruzzo produces organic wines from the Abruzzo region.

552. Best recent vintages for central Italy were 1999, 2000, 2001, and 2004.

WINES OF SOUTHERN ITALY AND THE ISLANDS

553. While traditionally a sweet wine center, Sicily is fast becoming recognized for its dry wines from modern producers who make IGT and VDT wines from international and local varieties. Watch for wines from the excellent Regaleali estate.

554. The Campania region is known for its Fiano di Avellino wine, which is a dry white with the distinct flavor of hazelnuts.

555. Greco di Tufo and Taurasi are wines worth tasting from Campania. Greco di Tufo is a white wine from the Greco grape, reminiscent of lime. Taurasi is a full-bodied red made from the Aglianico grape that must be aged for three years—including one in wood—before release. Taurasi can taste much like burnt cherries.

556. Feudi di San Gregorio is an estate that makes first-class Greco di Tufo.

557. Mastroberardino makes a good Taurasi that tastes of violet, smoky cherries, and black pepper.

558. Terradora di Paolo is a fine producer of Aglianico-based wines from Campania. Its 2004 Aglianico d'Irpina shows layers of melting dark chocolate, smoke, cherries, and leather.

559. The island of Sardinia makes some brilliant wines from local grape varieties. The Nuragus grape is found almost exclusively here and yields a lovely crisp, lemony wine. The Dolianova winery makes a spirited Nuragus in its Dolia range. This wine starts shy with a quiet nose of white flowers and then becomes quite vivacious on the palate with bright lemons that take me back to the Mediterranean coast instantly.

560. Cannonau is a local red grape from Sardinia that can make delicious wines that exude herbs, blackberries, and spice. Turriga IGT is a Cannonau-based wine that is simply stellar by a producer called Argiolas. Though vintages vary, the hallmark flavors tend to be oregano and lavender, blackberries and blueberries, truffle and tobacco. The wines almost caress the palate. Gambero Rosso, Italy's leading wine guide, has awarded past vintages of this wine the coveted *Tre Bicchieri*—or three glass status.

561. Cantina Sociale Santadi is a cooperative on the island of Sardinia that produces excellent wines. Santadi's Carignan-based Terre Brune wine is quite a sought after and nuanced wine of juicy plum, wild blueberry, aromatic bay leaf, tobacco, rich chocolate, black pepper, and seriously ripe raspberries.

562. Sardo restaurant in the heart of London, England, specializes in Sardinian wines and cuisine. Good food and drink at reasonable prices make it worth a visit when you're in that town.

11.

Spanish Wine

WINES OF RIOJA

563. Red wines from Rioja are made mainly from Garnacha and Tempranillo grapes, and are usually aged in American oak. The result is a wine that tastes of warm mixed berries, toasty oak, and vanilla.

564. That vanilla-scent that rises from glasses of Rioja reds comes from time spent in American oak before bottling. Some producers are now changing to French oak barrels for aging the wine, which results in a wine with a spicier perfume.

565. A treasure from this region is a wine called Hiru Tres Racimos by Bodegas Luis Cañas. It's a red wine of deep concentration that is made from eighty-year-old vines that yield just three bunches of grapes each. Older vines produce more complex wines and low yields—and three bunches is very low—mean concentration. Sensational stuff.

566. Other top producers in Rioja include Marqués de Murrieta, Bodegas Palacios Remondo, Marqués de Riscal, Artadi, Finca Allende, Viña Izadi, Luís Cañas, Primicia, and Roda.

567. Marqués de Riscal's Red Reserva delivers consistently outstanding value. It is a wine that is at once mouth-filling, yet refined. Cinnamon and spice, ripe blueberries and raspberries, silky smooth smoke and chocolate, and hints of caramel and vanilla are all in this wine. Look for the bottle plastered with its distinctive white and gold label and enmeshed in gold thread. Dirt cheap for what it has to offer.

568. Marqués de Murrieta's Dalmau Tinto Reserva is a big red wine that tastes of supersweet strawberries and raspberries, rich cocoa, and smoky vanilla. Quite an intense wine with considerable length.

569. Traditional white Rioja wines aren't easy to come by, and they offer a style you either love or hate due to a slightly oxidized character, which is intentional. For a prototype, try Marqués de Murrieta's Blanco Reserva. It's made from the Viura grape and is aged in American oak for almost two years. The result is a full-bodied dry wine that's deep in color, and tastes of ripe apricots, butterscotch, vanilla, and nuts. I must confess, I love it.

570. Opposite to the style of the traditional white noted above is the Blanco Seco by Marqués de Cáceres. Also made from Viura grapes, it's a modern, fresh, fruity wine that's lighter bodied and relatively inexpensive. In general, wines by Marqués de Cáceres are slightly more modern and show less oak than those from more traditional bodegas.

571. Perhaps the most brilliant winemaker in Rioja, if not all of Spain, is Alvaro Palacios. His passion for quality is reflected in three wines from his Rioja winery, Bodegas Palacios Remondo—La Vendimia, La Montessa, and the magical Propiedad.

572. La Vendimia 2004 is a bright, vivacious Rioja bursting with exuberant flavors of raspberry, blueberry, and pepper spice. The wine is beautifully balanced, friendly, and ready to drink.

573. La Montesa 2003 is round, soft, and plump with fine tannins and good weight. Velvety and lush on the tongue, this wine brims with roasted plum and black cherry flavors mingling with a bit of smoke and spice. It is drinking very well now.

574. And the top wine from Bodegas Palacios Remondo is the grandly unique Propiedad. The 2003 is a wine to hunt down, cherish, and cellar. A quietly impressive nose leads to a firm core layered with flavor after resounding flavor. Provencal herbs, smoke, tobacco, fine dark chocolate, cinnamon, caramel, toast, cherries and raspberry jam, and again rich, pure, melted chocolate. With this depth of flavor, along with a structure that will allow the wine to mature until about 2016, expect very good things to come. It is a serious wine offering extraordinary value for the money.

575. Winemaker Alvaro Palacios believes organic grape growing is critical to producing quality wine. The self-proclaimed quality fanatic says, "having life in the soil is the most important thing about making quality wine, and pesticides and fungicides take life out of the soil." This sentiment is echoed by many organic growers throughout the world.

576. Remelluri (pronounced ray-may-yoo-ree) is an organic producer in Rioja.

577. The 2001 vintage in Rioja was the best one in years, with excellent weather conditions yielding healthy grapes. Other very good recent vintages were 2003 and 2004, though not quite as stellar as 2001.

WINES OF RIBERA DEL DUERO

578. Ribera del Duero is home to some of Spain's most stylish red wines of the moment. Quality producers to look for include Vega Sicilia, Bodegas Pesquera, Bodegas Ismael Arroyo, and Dominio de Pingus.

579. Vega Sicilia's flagship wine, Único, is widely regarded as one of the best wines from Spain today. Único is released after ten years aging in oak and bottle, and it is a wine made only in the very best years. It is mainly Tinto Fino—Ribera del Duero's local variety of Tempranillo—with smaller proportions of Cabernet Sauvignon, Merlot, and Malbec.

580. Vega Sicilia was the first winery in the region to earn international recognition for its outstanding wines. Now, some of the better wineries of this region are following suit and making wine from Tinto Fino blended with the international varieties Cabernet Sauvignon, Merlot, and Malbec.

581. Domino de Pingus in the Ribera del Duero and Quinta Sardonia just outside of the region in Sardon del Duero both produce organic wines.

582. The region of Ribera del Duero does make white wine but it's rarely exported.

583. Best recent vintages include 2000, 2001, 2002, and 2003.

WINES OF NORTHEAST SPAIN

584. Cava comes from Catalonia in Northeastern Spain. Cava is a dry white fizz made bubbly the same way as Champagne, by inducing a second fermentation in the bottle.

585. Cava is made from a blend of Macabeo, Parellada, Xarel-lo, and sometimes Chardonnay grapes, which is why it tastes nothing like Champagne. The famous French fizz is made from Chardonnay, Pinot Noir, and Pinot Meunier.

586. The two biggest producers of Cava are Freixenet and Codorníu, the latter of which is arguably the better of the two. Codorníu's Raventos Brut is all grapefruit and fresh flowers with Cava's typical hint of earthiness on the finish.

587. Priorat is a trendy Spanish wine from an area of the same name in Northeastern Spain. In the late 1980s, a handful of pioneering winemakers applied modern techniques to the fruit of ancient vineyards to create concentrated, high-quality red wines from Garnacha, Cariñena, Cabernet Sauvignon, Merlot, and Syrah.

588. Top Priorat wines include Clos Mogador, Clos Martinet, Clos de l'Obac, Clos Erasmus, Clos Dofi (renamed Finca Dofi in 1994), L'Ermita, and Les Terrasses. They're excellent quality, ageworthy, and fairly expensive.

589. The wines L'Ermita, Finca Dofi, and Les Terrasses are made by Alvaro Palacios, the celebrated winemaker who put Priorat on the map. He's also linked with his family's Rioja winery, Bodegas Palacios Remondo.

590. The 2003 Les Terrasses is a complex wine that slowly reveals itself in the mouth with layers of black cherry, tobacco, cocoa, warm stones, and spice flavors. A very alluring wine.

591. The Navara region in Northeast Spain produces a cheerful pink wine called Gran Feudo by Bodegas J. Chivite. Strawberries, red apple, and fresh bread aromas lead to a delicious palate of ripe summer berries. This is a crowd-pleasing, afternoon-in-the-sunshine drink to have chilled with a plate of spicy Chorizo sausage.

592. Albet i Noya, Mas Estela, and Bodegas Lezaun are organic producers in Northeast Spain.

593. The best recent vintages for the region include 1999, 2000, 2001, 2003, and 2004.

WINES OF NORTHWEST SPAIN

594. Northwestern Spain is for white wine lovers. Particularly good white wines from the region are made from Albariño and Verdejo grape varieties.

595. If you like Riesling, you'll love Albariño—a Spanish wine made from a grape of the same name. It's aromatic and crisp yet delicate, reminiscent of green apples and herbs, and resonates with layers of other flavors such as coconut and pineapple depending on the winemaker. Adegas Morgadío makes one with aromas of pineapple, peach, orange, coconut, and a general palate-pleasing sumptuousness. Captivating.

596. Rias Baixas in Northwest Spain is known for producing excellent Albariño wine.

597. Martin Códax makes a very fine Albariño from Rias Baixas called Burgáns. The 2004 is everything this style of wine should be—full and fresh with clean lemon oil, apricot, and green apples on the palate and a long, graceful mineral finish.

598. Verdejo is a good quality white wine grape from the Rueda region in Northwest Spain. Verdejo-based wines taste of lemon, herbs, and nuts and are often blended with Sauvignon Blanc for body.

599. Verdejo offers very good value for the price with many bottles costing less than $10. A reliable producer is Marqués de Riscal; their Rueda Blanco is 85 percent Verdejo and 15 percent Viura and reveals sprightly lemon fruit with hints of spiced nuts.

600. Another shining example of Verdejo from the Ruedo region is Palacio de Menade 2004, which is aromatic and crisp, long, and focused with flavors of gentle herbs, lemon, and tropical fruit. Outstanding value at under $10.

601. Despite the fact Northwest Spain sings to white wine lovers, there are some decidedly tasty reds. Descendientes de Jose Palacios, a biodynamic property in the Bierzo region, makes an intense and serious sipper named Petalos del Bierzo. It tastes of red bell pepper, forest fruits, herbs, and spice, delivering a lengthy finish of black pepper and smoke. This is a very handsome wine at a remarkably reasonable price.

602. The wines from Descendientes de Jose Palacios are made by Alvaro Palacios, the celebrated winemaker who put Priorat on the map in the Northeast of the country by making such sought after wines as L'Ermita and its sister wines Finca Dofi and Les Terrasses.

603. All wines by Alvaro Palacios are organic, dark, wild-eyed beauties, but you won't see the "o" word on the label because he thinks a wine's quality should speak for itself.

604. In Rias Baixes, there hasn't been an above average vintage since 1997, while Bierzo has had many great vintages recently, including 2000, 2001, 2002, and 2004.

WINES OF CENTRAL AND SOUTHERN SPAIN

605. Almansa is a region about thirty-seven miles inland from Valencia. One company dominates the quality wine production there—Bodegas Piqueras. It produces wines under the label Castillo de Almansa. The Tinto Reserva is all fresh berries, leather, dried fruit, and spice in a glass. At about $10 a bottle, this wine delivers serious value.

606. La Mancha—a huge region in central Spain—produces very average wines, most of which don't compete well internationally. The area is progressing, but slowly.

607. Some good deals can be found with red wines from southern Spain if you know where to look. Red wines from Jumilla in southern Spain by Bodegas Casa Castillo for instance offer very good value at about $10 a bottle.

608. Jumilla's best recent vintages were 1999, 2000, and 2003.

SHERRY

609. Let it first be said that Sherry only comes from one place in the world—the Jerez region of Southwestern Spain. This is the most important thing about Sherry. The second most important fact is that it's out of fashion, underappreciated, and seriously undervalued.

610. The name Sherry is thought to be the English corruption of the region where this fortified wine is made—Jerez.

611. Sherry is made from three white grape varieties—Palomino, Pedro Ximénez, and Moscatel. Sherry can be made from just one of these varieties, but they're usually blended for balance and complexity.

612. All Sherry is either Fino or Oloroso, or a descendent of these two types.

613. Fino Sherry is generally bone dry. Its distinctive bread-like character comes from a yeast film called flor that develops on the wine's surface as it is being made. The flor protects the Fino from oxidizing and keeps it delicate and fresh.

614. Tío Pepe by González Byass is a classic example of a Fino—bone dry and very neutral with a slightly salty tang and hints of fresh bread. Not a fruity drink.

615. An Amontillado Sherry is a Fino that has lost its flor and has thus become amber and oxidized, which is intentional of course. True Amontillados are bone dry, but some producers sweeten them—read the back label to be sure of sugar levels.

616. Hidalgo makes an excellent Amontillado called Napoleon Seco that's all coffee, toffee, and nuts.

617. Manzanilla is dry Fino Sherry made in the seaside Spanish town of Sanlucar de Barrameda in Jerez. It tastes a bit salty, which has nothing to do with the fact that it's by the sea, but this is a handy way to remember the style.

618. Oloroso Sherries are dark brown, rich wines that have not been affected by a layer of flor yeast. As a result, they don't show that yeasty, bread-like character of Fino Sherry. Olorosos are fortified to 18 percent alcohol and they gain concentration as they age in cask. Traditional Oloroso Sherries are bone dry but today many producers sweeten them.

619. Pedro Domecq makes a dry Oloroso called Río Viejo, which tastes of nuts and brown sugar without any sweetness.

620. "Cream" Sherries are simply sweetened Olorosos. The exception is Harvey's Bristol Cream, which is a blend of Fino, Amontillado, and Oloroso Sherry, sweetened with Pedro Ximénez wine. This is the world's bestselling Sherry and delivers good value despite its reputation for being a bit old-fashioned. It tastes of raisins, nuts, orange rind, and toffee. Best drank on the rocks in front of a roaring fire on a cold evening before or after dinner.

621. Pedro Ximénez Sherry, known as PX, is an extremely sweet syrupy style best drizzled over vanilla ice cream.

622. A steady decline in sales since about 1980 has burdened the Sherry industry, prompting measures to improve its wines and rebuild its reputation. What does this mean? It's a good time to get reacquainted with this seriously undervalued wine.

623. Perhaps the most significant development of late is the four-year accord among growers, producers, and shippers in the Sherry region signed in September 2002. The agreement restricts production and reduces Sherry stocks to control supply, which generally means only the better quality stuff will end up on shelves. The accord also fixes grape prices that have been falling and intensifies promotional activity, which should mean that it will be easier to learn about Sherry.

624. As of year 2000, Sherry more than twenty years old could be labeled as "VOS" and those more than thirty years old as "VORS." The former is an acronym for the Latin "vinum optimum signatum" as well as "very old Sherry," and the latter stands for "vinum optimum rare signatum" as well as "very old rare Sherry." If you see these letters on a label, you can be assured of quality, as they would have been tasted blind to assess the average age and confirm the quality. The dating process provides quantifiable credibility to fine old Sherries. A similar system of certification is being considered for eight-, ten-, twelve-, and fifteen-year-old Sherry wines.

625. Some Sherry producers are introducing vintage wines to expand the premium end of their range. Vintage Sherries, which would of course mean those produced in a single year, are controversial because blending is so integral to the production of these fortified wines. Essentially, Sherry is made via an intricate system of fractional blending called a solera system, so removing this process takes away a bit of the wine's soul. Regardless, Williams & Humbert, González Byass, and Lustau have all started producing single vintage Sherries.

626. Within Lustau's Almacenista range are unique, artisan Sherry wines worth tasting.

627. A small but leading Sherry producer is El Maestro Sierra. If you see their wines, snap them up. This house's full range is outstanding, crowned by the Oloroso Jerez Extra Viejo 1/7.

628. Look to Barbadillo, Domecq, Emilio Lustau, and Hidalgo for Sherries of reliable quality.

629. Sherries tend to become higher in alcohol with time in cask. This curious fact is because of the unique conditions in Jerez cellars whereby water—not alcohol—is lost over time, so it's not uncommon to find old Olorosos with alcohol levels nearing 25 percent.

630. Once a Sherry has been bottled, it stops improving and starts to deteriorate. The dry Finos and Manzanilla styles go downhill quickest so buy these from a busy merchant with fast turnover. Heavier Olorosos, particularly the sweeter ones, keep best.

631. Sherry is an excellent start or end to a meal. Finos with olives to start and Olorosos with nuts or cheese to finish.

632. Since Sherry is usually a blend of wines from different years, vintage tends not to matter to these wines. The exception of course is in the case of vintage Sherries, which as noted above, is a new phenomenon.

12.

Portuguese Wine

WINES OF PORTUGAL

633. Portugal is starting to make some stunning dry red wines, particularly from the Douro, but also from the Alentejo, Estremadura, and the Ribatejo regions. As a result, it's shedding its image as simply a place to look for Port.

634. Barca Velha is one of Portugal's most famous and most expensive red wines. It sells in the U.S. for about $80 per bottle and comes from the Douro. It's regarded as Portugal's first great wine and had its initial vintage in 1952. Barca Velha is released ready to drink rather than cellar, and is made mainly from Tempranillo grapes—called Tinta Roriz in Portugal—blended with the traditional Port varieties of Tinta Borroca and Touriga Nacional.

635. Barca Velha varies slightly vintage to vintage, like a top-flight Bordeaux wine, but carries the hallmarks of intense berry fruit, spice, earth, chocolate, and smoke.

636. The 2001 Altano Reserva Douro is an excellent wine from the Douro region. It is a blend of the two Portuguese native grapes—Touriga Nacional and Touriga Franca—and is oak aged, creating a wine of ripe cherry, berry, and vanilla bean flavors.

637. The dry wines from the Douro tend to be made from the same varieties as those that go into Port, such as Tinta Roriz, Touriga Nacional, and Touriga Franca.

638. Sogrape is Portugal's largest wine company and its quality ranges from very average wine, such as its ubiquitous sweetish Mateus Rosé, to its better reds, such as the beautiful, silky, intense Reserva Alentejo. This red is a very seductive wine that sells at a mouthwatering price of under $20.

639. Another excellent producer from Portugal's Alentejo region is Cortes de Cima. The wines made at this family estate range from the Touriga Nacional 2003, which tastes of roses, violets, dark berries, and spice, to the wine called Hans Christian Andersen, made from 100 percent handpicked Syrah grapes. The 2005 vintage of this latter wine is all ripe plum, cherry-vanilla, and spice, but will develop more complexity in bottle as it matures.

640. DFJ Vinhos produces good quality wines from the Estremadura and Ribatejo regions of Portugal—at good prices.

641. Another stellar producer from Portugal is João Portugal Ramos. His wines are quite cutting edge, with the Marquês de Borba 2003 offering amazing value at less than $15. Bright red fruit, coffee, and spice. Long.

642. Although Portugal is not known for great white wines, it does make a quaffable, inexpensive white refresher called Vinho Verde. This name translates literally to green wine, with reference to the fact the wine is meant to be drank young—within a year of vintage ideally. Although it can be red as well as white, only the whites seem to hit export markets. Expect this wine to be floral, bone dry, tart, and lean, and often displaying a light sparkle. Sogrape is a reliable producer.

643. On a Portuguese wine label, the word *quinta* means estate, *casta* means grape variety, and *seco* means dry. *Doce* means sweet, *vinho* means wine, and *tinto* means red.

644. Portugal enjoyed excellent vintages in 2000, 2001, 2002, and 2004.

PORT

645. You can still hold strong to that romantic vision of Port being made by people treading on grapes in big stone vats called *lagares*. In fact, the first two-hour shift is spent marching, followed by a couple hours of dancing to music, which generally goes well into the night.

646. Robotic lagares and automated plungers have been replacing people treading grapes since the 1990s, but foot treading is still done by larger producers for premium vintage Ports, as well as by the smaller and more traditional houses.

647. Port is essentially a very potent sweet wine. It's made by fermenting crushed grapes to 6 to 9 percent alcohol, and then adding grape spirit, which raises the alcohol level to about 20 percent alcohol by volume, killing the yeast and stopping fermentation. Because the yeasts are killed before they can transform all the grape sugar into alcohol, the wine remains sweet.

648. Most Port is made from red grapes but occasionally white Ports are made. White Port is made from white grapes and looks golden in color from time in cask.

649. Tawny Port is amber colored and can be made two ways. Less expensive tawnies are made by blending young red and white Port, and are recognizable by a pink rim. Better Tawnies are made only from red Port that has been aged in oak casks for long periods of time before bottling, and are recognizable by a russet-colored rim—and steeper prices.

650. The very best Tawny Ports indicate their age of the wine on the label—ten, twenty, thirty, or over forty years are standard—as well as the year of bottling. These wines will not throw sediment so there is no need to decant them for this purpose. Decanting will give the wines air though, and is a smart move if you want to drink the whole bottle at one sitting. Left without decanting, the wine should last a few weeks in bottle.

651. A twenty-year-old Port arguably offers the best value because it combines the complexity of age without the vigor of youth.

652. A good Port tastes sweet but finishes dry. This means there's no cloying sweetness after the swallow because of the wine's intrinsic tartness that makes you salivate and cleanses the palate. Sweetness in wine hides acidity, so Port will never actually seem sour.

653. Ruby Port is a young, nonvintage, fortified wine that is generally bottled and sold after spending three years in cask. It's inexpensive, fruity, and popular.

654. If a Ruby Port label reads *reserve*, it has been aged in oak for about six years before being bottled and sold. Reserve Rubies are more complex and harmonious than a simple Ruby.

655. If you like Vintage Port but don't want to pay the price for this most premium selection, buy either Crusted Port or Late-Bottled Vintage Port.

656. Crusted Port is a ripe Ruby style that throws a sediment so, like Vintage Port, it needs decanting. Crusted and Vintage Port are both bottled unfiltered to let all the flavorful bits continue to infuse character into the wine in bottle. Yet, unlike Vintage Port, Crusted doesn't show a vintage on the label because it's generally a blend from different years, is ready to drink by the time it hits the shelves, and is relatively inexpensive.

657. Late-Bottled Vintage Port (LBV) is one step up from Crusted Port quality-wise, having spent a couple of extra years in cask. LBV is bottled unfiltered and throws a sediment but, unlike Crusted Port, it shows a year on its label—much like Vintage Port.

658. LBV can come filtered—such as Taylor's version, which doesn't require decanting.

659. LBV will keep a few weeks after opening if not decanted. Decanting exposes the wine to oxygen, decreasing the amount of time the wine stays fresh.

660. Colheita Port is a fine Tawny Port of a single vintage, aged in cask for at least eight years before release in bottle. It doesn't throw sediment so don't worry about decanting it for this purpose.

661. Vintage Port is produced only in exceptionally good years, and is generally produced from fruit of the best vineyards. Not all houses agree on what years are extraordinary though so Vintage Port years can vary by producer. Vintage Port is the most expensive style of Port you can buy.

662. 1985 was an outstanding year for Vintage Port, and was declared almost unanimously among producers.

663. Vintage Port is bottled when it is two years old and ages in bottle for years. It shouldn't really be drank for at least fifteen years from the vintage date, and during this time it will develop great complexity and depth of flavor. This is the joy of the wine and the reason for its steep price. Because it ages in bottle and is an unfiltered red wine, it will need decanting to separate the wine from the sediment.

664. Single Quinta Vintage Port is a wine made from the fruit of a single vineyard in a declared year. These are the cream of the crop of the Port world.

665. When decanting Vintage Port, you might consider using a sieve because the nature of the sediment is flakier than that of an old unfortified red wine.

666. Good years for Vintage Port recently were 1997, 2000, and 2003.

MADEIRA

667. Madeira is a fortified wine made on an island of the same name off the coast of Morocco. It is a province of Portugal.

668. Madeira comes in four styles: Sercial (dry—though not bone dry), Verdelho (off-dry), Bual (medium-sweet), and Malmsey (sweet).

669. Henriques & Henriques makes heart-warming Madeira. The Sercial is all toast and caramel, nuts, and dried fruit, resonating calmingly on the palate. It's my favorite fortified wine right now.

670. Madeira is the only wine that can be kept open indefinitely without losing character or finesse due to how it's made. Winemakers bake this fortified wine slowly—a process called estufagem—in open casks. This process caramelizes the sugars and oxidizes the wine intentionally, creating a characteristic caramelized flavor and a certain tang. The wines are often matured in casks after this process, resulting in nutty, toasty flavors and considerable complexity.

671. You know how long a bottle of Madeira has been aged in cask by a glance at the label. The word *reserve* means more than five years, *special reserve* means more than ten years, and *extra reserve* means more than fifteen years. So-called *vintage Madeira* must have spent at least twenty years in cask and two in bottle before release.

672. As with all wines, the longer Madeira is aged in cask, the more multifaceted it becomes. And the better quality the wine, the more cask aging it can withstand.

673. The grape varieties used in Madeira are Sercial, Verdelho, Bual, Malmsey, Tinta Negra Mole, Terrantez, and Bastardo.

13.

German Wine

674. The most important secret of German wine is that it is out of fashion and underappreciated, which means you can find very good wines from this country at excellent prices. And as in all wine regions, the best bottles come from the best producers.

675. German Riesling commanded higher prices than first-growth Bordeaux in the late nineteenth and early twentieth centuries. German wines were considered the finest wines of Europe, but they declined in quality in the twentieth century and are now fighting their way back to a reputable position on the world stage.

676. German wine tends to be fairly light, racheting up only about 9 percent alcohol by volume.

677. German wines are generally light in alcohol because the climate is cold. In cold climates, grapes ripen less, developing less sugar for the yeast to convert to alcohol. The cooler conditions also create grapes and wines with higher levels of natural acidity—or sourness. Of course a wine's grape variety or blend also influences its final acidity levels.

678. The wines of Germany are mainly white and often show some sweetness. However, bone dry wines are increasingly available, particularly at the higher price points.

679. The word *trocken* appears on the labels of dry wines while the word *halbtrocken* is noted on those that are off-dry—or just slightly sweet. If neither trocken nor halbtrocken appear on a label, it's safe to assume the wine is sweet.

680. Wines labeled with the word trockenbeerenauslese are the German equivalent of the sweet wines of Sauternes in France. The grapes will have been affected by noble rot, imparting that delicious marmalade character on the palate. These wines age beautifully, and are often sold in half bottles. German trockenbeerenauslese wines are more affordable than their French counterparts, and are usually of very good quality. I can't think of a more charming gift.

681. Wines labeled auslese or beere-nauslese will be sweet, with the former sweeter than the latter, but not as concentrated and luscious as trockenbeerenauslese.

682. Auslese and beerenauslese wines are often made from fruit affected by noble rot—called edelfäule in Germany.

683. Eiswein is the German equivalent of Canadian ice wine. These wines are made by pressing frozen grapes so the water remains in the form of ice crystals and the juice pressed is a thick nectar-like substance that's incredibly sweet, as is the resulting wine. However, unlike other sweet wines of Germany, these wines rarely show the lovely marmalade character imparted by noble rot.

684. Almost all wine produced in Germany notes the grape from which it's made on the label. Get to know a few German grapes and quality producers and you'll be well on your way to buying satisfying German wine.

685. If a grape appears on the label of a German wine, it must be made from at least 85 percent of that variety by law. If a vintage appears on the label, at least 85 percent of the fruit from which it's made must have been grown that year.

686. The main white grapes of Germany are Riesling, Müller-Thurgau, Silvaner, Kerner, Scheurebe, and Ruländer (known in France as Pinot Gris). The red varieties include Spätburgunder (aka Pinot Noir), Portugieser, Trollinger, and Dornfelder.

687. Riesling is generally regarded as Germany's best white wine. German Riesling ages well, and an aged Riesling exudes the unmistakable aroma of gasoline.

688. Weingut Max Ferd Richter is a three-hundred-year-old, family-owned estate in the Mosel area, and a leading producer of Riesling. Its classic dry Riesling generally displays flavors of crisp Granny Smith apples, lime zest, and warm stones. It's deliciously long with a tight, firm mouthfeel.

689. Wegeler Estate Riesling 2002 is another example of a fine Mosel wine, with aromas and flavors of peach, candied lime peel, apricot, and hints of passion fruit. It is off-dry and beautifully balanced, with a seam of good lime-squirt acidity to balance the touch of sweetness. It will develop nicely in bottle until about 2010.

690. Reliable producers of German wine include Bürklin-Wolf from the Pfalz, Schäfer-Fröhlich from the Nahe, and Loosen from the Mosel.

691. A full 60 percent of German wine exported is liebraumilch, which is a sweet, crisp, low alcohol, pretty average white wine. Blue Nun and Black Tower are two major brands of liebraumilch.

692. A few German producers have taken the road less traveled and decided to produce organic wine. Look for these names: Eymann, Schloss Wallhaüsen, and Sander.

693. Estates in Germany following biodynamic grapegrowing methods include Freiherr Heyl zu Herrnsheim, Hahnmülle, and Wittmann.

694. All of the years from 2001 to 2004 have been good vintages for German wine.

695. 2003 was a particularly great year for German Rieslings, but relatively little wine was made. If you find it, and it's made by a reputable producer, buy it.

14.

Austrian Wine

696. Austria makes very good dry white wine, particularly from Grüner Veltliner, Pinot Blanc, and Riesling grapes.

697. Grüner Veltliner is usually bone dry, very crisp, and tastes of fresh lime. It's Austria's flagship grape variety and one of my favorite summer refreshers.

698. Weingut Brundlemayer is an excellent producer from the Kamptal region. Its Riesling Heiligenstein Alte Reben 2002 is outstanding. Restrained nose of soft lime. On the palate: minerals and lime, oranges and lemon, cashews and almonds. Deliberate and rich.

699. The Riesling Steinmassel 2002 by Weingut Brundlemayer is delicious. Apple and mineral nose with bright lime and orange flavors, some tropical fruit, and nuttiness. Great energy balanced with a soft sensual mouthfeel.

700. Dr. Unger is a high quality producer that makes stunning wines in the Kremstal region. His 2002 Riesling Reserve shows considerable restraint on the nose with the faintest suggestion of peaches before it attacks the palate with lime juice, cooked peaches, and bright kiwi fruit flavors. Crisp and dry. On the finish, an obvious flavor of white pepper resonates. At 13.5 percent alcohol, this is a full-bodied wine and one to pair with food. Salmon in pastry would be perfect.

701. Some of the best Austrian Rieslings come from the Wachau region.

702. Austria makes excellent sweet wines with racy, cleansing acidity.

703. *Extratrocken*, *trocken*, *halbtrocken*, *süss*, *beerenauslese* (BA), and *trockenbeerenauslese* are terms that can appear on an Austrian wine label to indicate increasing levels of sweetness. *Extratrocken* means bone dry and a *trockenbeerenauslese (TBA)* is lusciously sweet from grapes shriveled by botrytis.

704. Austrian BA and TBA are less expensive than their German counterparts, and much less so than Sauternes. They offer great value.

705. Burgenland is the most important sweet wine region in Austria. The sweet wines from Burgenland are made from fruit affected by noble rot, so expect that wonderfully succulent marmalade character similar to wines from Sauternes and Barsac in France.

706. Weingut Geyerhof produces organic wines.

707. Nikolaihof Wachau and Weingut Schön-berger are biodynamic producers.

708. Best recent vintages were 1999, 2000, 2002, 2003, and 2004 for Austrian wine.

15.

Swiss Wine

709. Overall, about half of all Swiss wine is red and the other half is white. Chasselas is the main white grape variety of Switzerland, but Müller-Thurgau (locally called Riesling-Sylvaner) and Sylvaner are also widely produced. Blauburgunder (Pinot Noir) is the main red of Switzerland, while Gamay and Merlot are also grown in large quantity.

710. As well as the familiar grape varieties grown internationally, Switzerland grows an astounding forty indigenous varieties, many of which aren't grown anywhere else in the world.

711. Swiss wines tend to be lower in acidity—less sour—and higher in alcohol than their German and Austrian counterparts.

712. Swiss wines are usually expensive, and not easily found outside of Switzerland, but they are being exported more each year. The top importers of Swiss red wine are Germany, the U.S., and France, while the leading importers of Swiss whites are Germany, Belgium, and France.

713. Domaine de Beudon is a certified biodynamic producer in Switzerland.

714. 2003 was a very good year for Swiss wine.

16.

Central and Eastern European Wine

715. The best wine coming out of central and eastern Europe is Tokaji Aszú, a sweet wine named after the town Tokaj in Hungary.

716. Tokaji is a wine-growing region in Hungary, and Aszú means noble rot. So wines labeled Tokaji Aszú are made from botrytis-affected grapes and are thus sweet. They display the characteristic flavors of apricot and marmalade, like those of Sauternes in France and Burgenland in Austria. It's worth bearing in mind that Tokaji produces dry and sweet wines so make sure the word *Aszú* appears on the label if you're looking for the sweet version.

717. The more "puttonyos" indicated on a bottle of Tokaji Aszú, the sweeter the wine. A minimum of three puttonyos and a maximum of six can appear on labels. Puttonyos comes from the word puttony, which was the name given to the portable troughs traditionally used to dump nobly rotten grapes into a barrel of dry base wine during the process of making Tokaji Aszú. The more puttonyos tipped in, the sweeter the resulting wine. Puttonies are no longer used of course, but the wine labels still reflect this tradition.

718. Beyond six puttonyos, an even sweeter wine called Aszú Eszencia exists, but it is very rare and seriously expensive.

719. The best producers of Tokaji Aszú are Szepsy and Királyudvar. Production levels are small, and the wines are expensive to produce and purchase, but the quality is outstanding.

720. Classic flavors of Tokaji Aszú are warm caramel, luscious apricot, and rich honey. Other sweet wines may be more popular, but this wine is often better.

721. The best recent vintages for Tokaji Aszú are 1995, 1999, 2000, and 2003.

722. Hungary also produces dry wine, notably from the Furmint grape. The wine tends to be crisp and taste of honey and apples.

723. The Bulgarian wine industry is trying to improve its quality and reputation. Today, the country's wine remains average at best compared to wine of the same price from other wine regions of the world.

724. Everything-he-touches-turns-to-gold wine consultant Michel Rolland has just added a Bulgarian winery to his client list. He is now working with Telish Wine Cellars in Northern Bulgaria to improve the quality of this producer's wines. Expect good things to come.

725. Movia in Slovenia is one of the few biodynamic and organic wine producers in Central and Eastern Europe.

17.

Mediterranean Wine

726. Despite Israel's constant political turmoil and poor image as a wine producer, it is starting to churn out some very good wine from two regions—Upper Galilee and the Judean Hills. The soil, altitude, and climate of these places create favorable grape growing conditions so winemakers have come to the area recently to craft high caliber wines.

727. A couple of leading Israeli wine producers include Domaine du Castel and the Golan Heights Winery. The former produces wines under the name Castel-Grand Vin, and the latter makes wines under the Yarden, Gamla, and Golan labels. Quality Israeli wines are a new phenomenon. Domaine du Castel's first crush took place in 1992, and the Golan Heights Winery launched its first wines in 1984.

728. Château Musar is the most famous wine of Lebanon. Located just fifteen miles from Beirut, political unrest creates winemaking challenges not all winemakers are forced to face (such as bombings), and yet Musar continues to produce reasonably good wine under the Château's own name.

729. Cyprus made wine six thousand years ago and was the first Mediterranean country to do so.

730. Although Greece makes wine from such international varieties as Cabernet Sauvignon, Sauvignon Blanc, Chardonnay, Syrah, and Viognier, it's worth looking for bottles that include the local variety, Assyrtiko. This is a white grape of lemony freshness and a mineral finish. The stony nuance is most pronounced when it's grown on the volcanic soil of Santorini.

731. Sigalas Paris is the leading wine-maker on the island of Santorini, producing a range of very interesting, rather exciting wines from organically grown grapes. His white wines made from 100 percent Assyrtiko come in oaked and unoaked styles. The wines of Sigalas Paris have a good balance of extract and tartness, with flavors and aromas of mixed citrus zest and the characteristic earth and mineral flavors derived from Santorini's soil. The oaked versions show well-integrated complexity from the wood.

732. Greek wine is not—and likely will never be—inexpensive. This is simply because producers are small and economies of scale dictate that production costs remain relatively high.

733. If you see a bottle of Greek wine called Retsina, bear in mind it is flavored with pine-resin and is usually a bit of an acquired taste.

18.

American Wine

WINES OF CALIFORNIA

734. Several Californian wines gained something of a cult status in the last couple of decades. These so-called cult wines rise above their peers on clouds of inflated reputations, puffed up by jovial zealots and excited wine critics. They usually carry—and often meet—high expectations, but prices tend to be very steep. The list of cult wines is rather nebulous and shifts year to year, but currently it is believed to include the wines of Araujo Eisele Vineyards, Bryant Family Vineyard, Colgin Cellars, Dalla Valle Vineyards, Grace Family Vineyards, Harlan Estate, Screaming Eagle Winery, and Shafer Vineyards. The prototype and nucleus of Californian cult wines is Screaming Eagle.

735. Screaming Eagle rose to cult status almost immediately when, after its first vintage in 1992, the powerful U.S. wine critic Robert Parker Jr. gave it 99 points out of 100, stirring a frenzy of demand for the mere 225 cases of the wine made that year. Now about six hundred cases are produced—though it varies vintage to vintage—and the only way to get some of this wine is by being on the winery's mailing list, for which there is a twelve year waiting list when this book went to print.

736. Each person on Screaming Eagle's mailing list is allotted three bottles at $300 each. From there, a handful of retailers buy the wine from auctions and resell it. You can buy the 2003 vintage, for instance, from The Saratoga Wine Exchange for $1,200 per bottle. At the 2000 Napa Valley Wine Auction, a six-liter bottle of Screaming Eagle's first vintage sold for $500,000.

737. In March 2006, Screaming Eagle Winery was sold to two financial entrepreneurs, Charles Banks and Stanley Kroenke. Hopefully the wine won't change with the new ownership. Banks told the *San Francisco Chronicle* shortly after he bought the winery that he has no plans to change the winemaker, Heidi Barrett, saying, "as long as she wants to be there, she will be there."

738. Heidi Barrett is an independent wine-maker who has made wine for such top-tier Napa clients as Screaming Eagle, Paradigm Winery, Dalla Valle Vineyards, Barbour Vineyards, Amuse Bouche Winery, Lamborn Family Vineyards, Showket Vineyards, Grace Family Vineyards, Silver Oak Cellars, Franciscan Estates, and Buehler Vineyards. Her latest client is Revana Family Vineyard. Plus, she recently started producing 1,500 cases of her own wine called La Sirena, a range that includes two Syrahs, a Cabernet Sauvignon, and a dry Muscat Canelli.

739. Dick Grace, owner of Grace Family Vineyards, gives hundreds of thousands of dollars in profit from his cult wines to children's charities in Nepal, Mexico, and India. Grace is a devout Buddhist. If you're wondering what his wine tastes like, the 2003 Grace Family Cabernet Sauvignon shows complex layers of spice, chocolate, cassis, black cherry, coffee, and herbs.

740. While California isn't generally known for its Sauvignon Blanc in the way that say, the Loire Valley in France and Marlborough in New Zealand are, this state does produce some very fine examples of this variety at surprisingly low prices. For about $10, Racho Zabaco's Dancing Bull Sauvignon 2004 is a great buy. In fact, its minerality and freshness is strikingly similar to Sauvignon Blanc from great parts of the Eastern Loire, such as Pouilly Fumé. Restrained asparagus, apple, and herb flavors swirl around a firm and intense stony core. This is very good wine that would make an ideal accompaniment to al fresco dining.

741. Only in California could stardom be intertwined with winedom. In 1974, Francis Ford and Eleanor Coppola used royalties from *The Godfather* movie to buy the Niebaum-Coppola Estate Winery and produce the flagship wine Rubicon. The wine was named after the river Julius Caesar crossed when he marched on Rome to seize power. Caesar knew once he crossed the Rubicon, there would be no turning back. Coppola said he knew once he sunk the royalties from *The Godfather* into the estate, there would be no turning back. Reassured he was on the right track by his neighbor and friend 'Bob' (Mondavi), two *Godfather* sequels have assured Rubicon's place in winemaking history.

742. Niebaum-Coppola Winery's recent gem is a little pink tin of bubbly. The wine is named Sofia Mini Blanc de Blancs after actress-director Sofia Coppola, daughter of Francis Ford Coppola. The wine is a blend of Pinot Blanc, Sauvignon Blanc, and Muscat, sells for about $20 for four cans, and tastes of citrus, apricots, tangerine, and pear. It's dry and fruity, aromatic, and, oh by the way, is one of Oprah Winfrey's favorite things.

743. In a groundbreaking blind tasting in 1976 in Paris, top Californian Cabernets beat leading wines of Bordeaux. This was a huge achievement that shook the foundations of the wine world and set the stage for California's ensuing success in the premium and super-premium wine market. At the tasting, Californian Cabernet Sauvignon wines, including Ridge Monte Bello 1971, Stag's Leap Wine Cellars 1973, Mayacamas 1971, Heitz 1970, and Clos du Val 1972, beat top-tier Bordeaux wines. The tasting was repeated in London in May 2006 and the results were amazing. Decanter.com reported "some of the world's most eminent tasters found the Californian wines to have retained more of their verve over the years than the Bordeaux."

744. The world is awash in mediocre Chardonnays so it is inspiring to find an exhilarating example that rings of the archetypal Chardonnay—white Burgundy. Estancia Estates' Pinnacles Chardonnay from Monterey is very Burgundian; it's all finesse and class with fine texture, great balance, gentle almond, and a subtle butteriness threaded with vanilla. What quickens the pulse is the price, which falls under $10. But drink up. It's not really made for aging.

745. Beringer White Zinfandel is a plumply-fruited, strawberry-scented pink wine that offers very good value for the money if you're looking for a crowd-pleasing quaffer to drink outside on a hot summer day. Rather cheap and quite cheerful.

746. Wines labeled Napa Gamay and Gamay Beaujolais are not truly made with Gamay grapes. Gamay Beaujolais is a clone of Pinot Noir, and the Napa Gamay is the Valdiguié grape of the French Midi region.

747. Although Pinot Noir is generally a cool climate grape, one Californian winery is doing an good job producing wines from this variety. At the Hartford Family Winery, Don and Jennifer Hartford make seven fine Pinot Noir wines from low-yielding vines grown on small sites in cool areas. The results are lovingly stitched expressions of the family's passion and understanding of this grape. The wines can be ordered online at www.hartfordwines.com.

748. California is the leading wine producing state in the U.S. Wine producing grapes are grown in forty-six of California's fifty-eight counties, covering 513,000 acres in 2004, according to the Wine Institute of California.

749. There are more than ninety-three American Viticultural Areas (AVAs) in California, which are wine grape growing areas recognized by the U.S. government—the equivalent of Europe's *appellations*. Official AVAs include areas such as Alexander Valley, Anderson Valley, Dry Creek Valley, El Dorado, Guenoc Valley, Howell Mountain, Lodi, Los Carneros, Malibu-Newton Canyon, Mendocino, Mendocino Ridge, and Monterey to name a handful.

750. California wines attract tourists. Wineries and vineyards are the second most popular tourist destination in California after Disneyland, with 14.8 million tourists visiting the state's wine regions each year.

751. Zinfandel is one of California's cornerstone grape varieties, producing wines that taste of blackberry, blueberry, and raspberry cordials with hints of peppercorn.

752. There's a phrase in the trade about blind tasting red wines that goes, "If it's red and it is sweet, it's probably Port." I was in Paris one day when the proprietor of a café delivered two glasses of red sweet wine to our table after lunch. We pondered what the delicious surprise might be and agreed it must be Port. Then, he showed us the bottle. It was Rosenblum Cellars' Late Harvest Zinfandel. I cannot recommend it highly enough. It was sun-drenched and ripe, yet well-balanced, chocolaty, and delicious.

753. Rosenblum Cellars makes a range of sweet delectable wines, including Late Harvest Zinfandel, Late Harvest Viognier, Zinfandel Port, Black Muscat, and the Désirée Chocolate Dessert Wine.

754. The leading producers of Zinfandel are Ravenswood and Rosenblum. Zinfandel is one of the best value red wines around today.

755. Well-made Zinfandel can age very well if given the chance. The best examples can actually improve for up to three decades.

756. Ravenswood Vintners Blend is always an easy-drinking, good value wine that tastes ripe, velvety, and sensually pleasurable at a mouthwatering price of less than $10. It is bottled ready to drink.

757. Among the vast range of Rosenblum Zinfandels, that from the Harris Kratka Vineyard in the Alexander Valley is especially interesting. The 2002 vintage tastes of raspberry, sweet cherry, violet, rose petal, vanilla, and cream.

758. The Seghesio Old Vine Zinfandel from Sonoma County is a classic Zin with ample intensity. Chewy tannins, very ripe raspberry and blackberry fruit, toast, and a wide range of herbs and spice flitting from sage to white pepper attack the palate. Not a weak wine. Eat with grilled foods.

759. Roederer Estate's Anderson Valley Brut is a beautiful sparkling wine from California. Owned by Louis Roederer, the makers of Cristal Champagne, Roederer Estate's Anderson Valley Brut tastes close to a very ripe, well-made French Champagne. It is, to my mind, the best sparkling wine available today and the closest thing you'll find to Champagne outside of that renowned French region. This sparkler displays some hallmarks of Louis Roederer's exquisite Champagnes—biscuity flavors, toasted brioche, cooked apple, and hints of nuts and butter. Fresh, elegant, and very refined.

760. Traditionally, vines were ready to be harvested when their grape sugar reached certain levels as measured by a refractometer. This tool is being cast aside by many winemakers, particularly in California, in favor of tasting the grape for something called phenolic ripeness. The argument is that other parts of the grape mature at different rates than sugar levels, such as skins, acidity, and tannins. So, to maximize overall ripeness, many Californian producers now rely on extended hang times, which means leaving fruit on the vines for days or weeks past the end of their growing cycles to increase overall ripeness.

761. Since the 1970s, Californian grapes have been picked progressively later to produce super-ripe, densely fruited wines that are high in extract and alcohol—a style that's become increasingly popular.

762. A backlash against the trend toward highly concentrated, alcoholic wines has begun to take form and pick up pace, particularly in Europe where these wines are viewed by some critics as inelegant, poor matches for food, and difficult to drink past a glass or so. Concentration, like so many style-related issues in wine, is a matter of personal taste.

763. So-called "*Terroir* expression" is taking hold in California as some quality minded growers are looking to rise above the masses to produce wines reflective of their small patches of origin.

764. Characteristic flavors of Cabernet Sauvignon produced in Paso Robles tend to be black raspberry, black cherry, cassis, tobacco, cedar, and dark chocolate. The wines from the area generally show ripe tannins, deep color, bright acidity, and opulent fruit intensity.

765. Mount Veeder produces ageworthy Cabernet Sauvignon wines high in tannins, rich in extract, and flashing with cassis, violets, aniseed, and dark chocolate.

766. Cabernet Sauvignon wines from Howell Mountain in Napa Valley express its terroir with aromas and flavors of raspberry, cassis, black pepper, and tobacco.

767. One of my favorite red wines these days from Napa is Opus One 1999. This stellar wine—born from a partnership between California's master, Mondavi, and the famous Bordeaux producer, Baron Philippe de Rothschild—tastes of leather and spice, coffee and chocolate, and masses of sweet black cherries, as well as cigar box and smoke. It is dense, deep, and delicious, but still has so much to give. It will age in bottle until about 2015. Perfect, seamless, and worth every one of the many pennies it costs.

768. The following wine producers practice organic viticulture: Araujo Estate Wines, Coturri Winery, Evasham Wood Winery, Fetzer Vineyard's Bonterra range, Frey Vineyards, Frogs Leap Winery, Patianna Organic Vineyards, and Robert Sinskey Vineyard.

769. Grace Family Vineyards, Bonterra Vineyards, Brick House Vineyards, Viader Vineyards & Winery, Grgich Hills, and the Benziger Family Winery all practice biodynamic viticulture. As noted earlier in the book, biodynamic viticulture is a way of farming that takes organic standards to a new level by working with the earth's spiritual energies. Does it make better wine? Interestingly, it often does.

770. Some of the best recent vintages for California were 2001, 2002, and 2003.

WINES OF OREGON, WASHINGTON, AND IDAHO

771. Oregon makes very good Pinot Noir. At best, this elixir is silky and perfumed, seductive and elegant. Pinot Noir is difficult to grow and only certain places in the world do it well. Oregon is one of them, and this grape variety is becoming the state's claim to fame in the wine world.

772. Pinot Noir from Oregon and elsewhere is distinguished because it is such a transparent medium for reflecting terroir. For this reason, the wines can be very different, but equally beautiful.

773. The Willamette Valley of Oregon, especially known for its Pinot Noir, is divided into six smaller regions, all of which produce their own expressions of this wine grape and its terroir. The regions include Dundee Hills, Eola Hills, Chehalem Mountains, Yamhill-Carlton District, Ribbon Ridge, and McMinnville. If you're into Oregon Pinot Noir, you can fine tune your passion further by zeroing in on one of these regions.

774. Dundee Hills makes Pinot Noir that tastes of raspberry, black cherry, earth, truffle, cola, and spice.

775. Eola Hills makes an amplified version of Pinot Noir. Blackberry, blueberry, black cherry, plum, and mineral flavors feature prominently, sometimes with suggestions of white pepper and dried flowers. These wines are fuller bodied and usually age well.

776. Chehalem Mountains makes a wide range of Pinot Noir from the brighter, raspberry-scented variety to the deeper, darker, black-fruited style depending on the exact vineyard location, weather, and producer.

777. Yamhill-Carlton District Pinot Noir tends to be mouth filling with complex flavors of red and black fruit, tobacco, coffee, clove, and smoke as well as violet, rose, and lavender.

778. McMinnville wines are highly pigmented for this notoriously pale red variety with a core of firm tannin and acidity, and a massive palate of fruit and earthiness.

779. Ribbon Ridge Pinot Noir tastes of black cherry, blackberry, and black currant, as well as earth, spice, and chocolate.

780. Washington makes world-class Riesling. Mosel winemaker Ernst Loosen and Chateau Ste. Michelle in Washington produce what is widely thought to be America's best Riesling—a wine called Eroica, named after Beethoven's masterpiece. It's a steal at less than $20 a bottle.

781. Chateau Ste. Michelle's Cabernet Sauvignon 2000 is a striking wine for the price. A creamy, black pepper, plum, and black currant nose followed by a rich, full palate of ripe, gripping tannins and balanced acidity. Generous mouthfeel. Best with meat or cheese to soften the tannins. Medium length. Very good value at about $10.

782. Chateau Ste. Michelle's Columbia Valley Chardonnay 2004 is classy, refined, and distinguished. It starts with aromas of coconut and lime, and broadens in the mouth with flavors of lush lime and mixed citrus fruit.

783. Washington's official American viticultural areas (AVAs) are Yakima Valley, Walla Walla Valley, Columbia Valley, Puget Sound, Red Mountain, Columbia Gorge, Horse Heaven Hills, and Wahluke Slope.

784. In 1996, Washington was home to eighty wineries. By 2006, there were more than four hundred.

785. Keep an eye out for wines by Zefina of Columbia Valley, Washington. A particularly noteworthy red wine called Serience Red is made from the Rhône varieties—Grenache, Syrah, and Mouvedre. This wine flashes with intrepid flavors of spice and leather, black pepper and plum, black cherry and smoke, tobacco and blood, finishing with spice, cherries, and smoke. Long. Compact and balanced.

786. Zefina also makes an excellent Zinfandel that tastes of chocolate and cherry, coffee and cinnamon.

787. Woodward Canyon Winery from the Walla Walla Valley in Washington is a reliable producer. Particularly delicious is the Artist Series Cabernet Sauvignon, exuding curious aromas of barbecued peppered steak followed by flavors of charred beef and red plums. A bit of wet stones and green pepper on the finish.

788. To my mind, some of the best wines from Washington come from L'Ecole No 41—a small family-run winery in a place called Frenchtown in Walla Walla, Washington. A favorite in their range is the 2001 vintage of the Seven Hills Merlot that displays caramelized meat drippings and marzipan on the nose, followed by an attack of marzipan, violets, black pepper, smoke, and berries on the palate. This is a complex and deeply satisfying wine. Long and delicious, with excellent structure. Watch for their Sémillons as well.

789. L'Ecole No 41 Cabernet Sauvignon 2001 is a classic beauty from twenty-five-year-old vines. The wine starts with ripe black currant fruit and roasted cashews on the nose, followed by lush lashings of spice, red berries, nuts, and black pepper on the palate. Gripping but ripe tannins. Long length.

790. Other reputable Washington producers to look for include Leonetti Cellar, Quilceda Creek Winery, Powers Winery, Pepper Bridge Winery, and Walla Walla Vintners.

791. Badger Mountain Vineyard is a producer of organic wines from Washington. The Mountain Vintners Estate Cabernet Sauvignon 1999 from this winery is superb, with aromas of black currant and spice leading to flavors of cinnamon, pepper, and black currant. This is a well-balanced, tight wine with ripe tannins that will soften with age. Very well made.

792. Idaho's first winery was founded in 1978. It was Ste. Chapelle, which to this day is the state's largest producer.

793. Idaho produces mainly Riesling, Chardonnay, and Pinot Noir—all hardier grapes that can withstand the icy Idaho winters. Since this cool region doesn't always produce fruit that ripens enough to make good quality still wine, the region also produces some sparklers from less ripe Chardonnay and Pinot Noir grapes.

794. Less than two dozen commercial wineries exist in Idaho today.

795. All vintages from 1997 to 2004 have been very good for Oregon Pinot Noir.

796. Best recent vintages in Washington were 2001, 2002, 2003, and 2004.

WINES OF NEW YORK STATE

797. The state of New York has four wine regions—the Finger Lakes, Lake Erie, Hudson River, and Long Island.

798. The Finger Lakes, Lake Erie, and Hudson River areas produce the best Chardonnay, Riesling, Gewürztraminer, and Pinot Blanc wines in New York state, as well as the finest Merlot and Cabernet Franc in the region.

799. Look to Long Island for Sauvignon Blanc and Cabernet Sauvignon wines. The growing conditions here match these grape varieties well.

800. The best Pinot Noir of New York state is made in the Hudson Valley and Finger Lakes areas.

801. New York state makes a lot of wines from hardy French hybrids, the best of which is probably Seyval Blanc. This grape makes dry and sometimes off-dry white wines reminiscent of grapefruit, green apple, and flowers.

802. New York State has just over two hundred wineries—a small fraction of California's 1,700 estates.

803. Leading producers from New York state include: Swedish Hill, Lamoreaux Landing Wine Cellars, Atwater Vineyards, Standing Stone Vineyards, Hermann J. Wiemer Vineyard, Diliberto Winery, Osprey's Dominion Vineyards, Chateau Lafayette Reneau Winery, and Pellegrini Winery and Vineyards.

804. Like Canada, New York state produces some very good late harvest and ice wines, both of which are sweet. One to look for is Casa Larga's Vidal Icewine called Fiori Delle Stelle; the 2004 tastes of pineapple and orange with hints of pure maple syrup.

WINES OF THE REST OF THE UNITED STATES

805. On May 16, 2005, the Supreme Court ruled that Americans can buy wines directly from out-of-state wineries—happy news for small vintners and wine enthusiasts alike. The new ruling struck down laws in New York state and Michigan that made it illegal to buy wines this way.

806. Fifty states in the United States make wine. Today, more than 3,700 wineries exist coast to coast, up from just 579 in 1975.

807. Wine from Virginia is making a name for itself with invigorating white wines. Wineries to watch include Rappahannock Cellars and Keswick Vineyards.

19.

Canadian Wine

808. Since wine grapevines grow best between 30–50° north and 30–50° south of the equator, it's surprising that Canada produces some fine quality wine with much of its land lying above 50° north latitude. It does so by taking advantage of more moderate microclimates. The major areas under vine include the Niagara region of Ontario and the Okanogan Valley of British Columbia, which are the two areas making the country's best quality wine, though smaller wine producing plots exist in almost every other province.

809. Canada has been making fine wine for less than fifty years. Inniskillin pioneered truly good quality wine in Ontario about thirty years ago. Compared with places in Europe that have been making it for centuries, Canada is still in its infancy.

810. Some major forces converged in the past few decades to improve the quality of Canadian wine. The 1988 Free Trade Agreement with the U.S. and the removal of protective laws favoring domestic wineries forced Canada to compete directly with American wineries. The most recent push for quality came with the creation of the Vintners Quality Alliance that set quality standards for Canadian wine. Ontario created VQA standards in 1988; British Columbia followed suit in 1990; and then VQA Canada was established in 1999. Almost all exported wine is VQA certified.

811. Recent improvements to Canadian wine stirred demand from other countries. In 2004, CAN$16 million worth of Canadian wine was exported; up from just CAN$6 million five years earlier. The most important export market by far is the United States, but Asia also buys a fair amount of Canadian wine.

812. When buying wine from Canada, make sure it is labeled VQA. It is the only way you can be sure it is made from 100 percent Canadian-grown grapes. If it is not labeled VQA, it may actually contain foreign juice and water.

813. Be wary of Ontario wine not labeled VQA from the 2005 vintage. In 2005, such wine could be made from as little as 1 percent Ontario-grown grapes, and have water added. The Ontario government laid down similar labeling law changes for the 2003 and 1993 vintages to off-set crop shortages. This situation is unfortunate for the Canadian consumer simply because this lesser quality wine is usually sold on shelves with other Canadian wines, including those which are VQA certified, which can be misleading.

814. One of Canada's best wineries is Burrowing Owl Estate Winery, which is VQA certified. Its most expensive wine, named Meritage, sells for Can$40 at the winery, and is a red blend of Bordeaux grape varieties. The 2003 vintage is delicious now, but will be even better in five years. Sweet red cherries, white pepper, blueberries, vanilla, milky chocolate, and a long black cherry finish. Fine tannins make the wine feel quite plush in the mouth.

815. St. Hubertus Estate Winery from British Columbia's Okanogan Valley produces some extraordinary white VQA wines, all of which are made from grapes grown with minimal use of pesticides, herbicides, and fungicides—always a plus in my book.

816. The 2005 Riesling from St. Hubertus Estates is an eloquent wine that could easily be confused with an Alsacean gem. It starts with a slowly enticing nose of flowers and candied lime, and leads to shifting flavors of delicate lilacs and white flowers, fresh limes, a certain steeliness, and a firm seam of minerality. It finishes bone dry and is huge fun to drink. Well done, Canada.

817. St. Hubertus Estate's 2005 Chasselas is a Canadian wine that would be a perfect outdoor aperitif. The sumptuous apricot aromas lead to a clean palate of ripe peaches and cream. Rich and concentrated, yet refreshing and tart. Good balance. Long and lovely.

818. Some of the better red wines of Canada are made from the Baco Noir grape, which makes deeply colored wines with low tannins and bright acidity. The flavors generally suggest black forest fruits and a bit of leather and spice. The Henry of Pelham Family Estate Winery makes some fine versions.

819. Canadian Icewines are highly regarded all over the world—particularly in Asia. The Icewine harvest starts when temperatures dip below about 14° Fahrenheit. Growers handpick and deliver frozen grapes to the winery for pressing. Since they're frozen, the water in the juice remains with the grape pulp in the form of ice crystals, and highly concentrated juice is expressed. This almost thick nectar results in a lusciously sweet wine.

820. Canadian Icewine is best served in stemware with a fairly large bowl. The stem lets you refrain from warming the wine with your fingers while you drink it, and the bowl amplifies the aromas and intensifies the flavors.

821. Some of the better Icewines are made from the hearty Vidal variety, but they're best drank within about five years of the vintage. Jackson-Triggs' 2003 Vidal Icewine is beautifully expressive with a nose of ripe pear and toasty marzipan, which leads to fresh, lively flavors of apricot, citrus, and almonds. Very clean, well-made wine with excellent concentration and length.

822. Inniskillin makes oaked and unoaked versions of Vidal Icewine. The oak aged one from 2003 is an example of how wood can lend a marvelous roasted nut character to the nose of tropical fruit. On the palate, toasted nuts appear again, along with mango chutney flavors. Good balance, concentration, and length. Lovely. Inniskillin's unoaked Vidal from the same vintage is also quite good. It begins with a nose of marzipan and orange with a hint of lemon zest, and then leads to a clean, bright attack on the palate with flavors of mixed citrus zest and subtle almonds. Very well-made, well-balanced, and long.

823. Icewines from Riesling are best for long-term cellaring. A leader is Henry of Pelham's 2003 version that starts with a buttery apple pie nose followed by a lusciously sweet palate of cooked juicy apple, citrus, and butterscotch. Will develop complexity with age.

824. Icewines from Cabernet Franc are made but I wouldn't recommend them over the whites because they tend to be one-dimensional wines reminiscent of candy apples.

825. Leading producers of Icewine include Henry of Pelham Family Estate Winery, Inniskillin, and Jackson-Triggs.

826. Canada also produces a lot of fruit wine, which is essentially wine made from fruit other than grapes. This drink is rarely exported, usually sweet though can be dry or off-dry, and must be drank as young as possible as it doesn't improve with age. Blossom Winery in British Columbia makes some fairly good ones. Its Eros Passion Fruit wine is off-dry, tart, and tastes of the fruit from which it is made.

827. Reliable producers of Canadian wine include Inniskillin, Cedarcreek Estate Winery, Jackson-Triggs, and Henry of Pelham Family Estate Winery.

828. Canada's largest certified organic vineyard is Summerhill Pyramid Winery in BC, and Feast of Fields Vineyards is Canada's only certified biodynamic grower.

829. The Liquor Control Board of Ontario, which controls the sale of all wine in that province, is the largest single purchaser of beverage alcohol in the world.

830. Ontario experienced a streak of very good vintages from 1997 to 2001. Particularly good years in British Columbia were 2001 and 2005.

20.

Chilean Wine

831. Merlot is the grape that made Chilean wines famous. In Chile's warm environment, Merlot makes deeply colored wines bursting with ripe, soft fruit.

832. Perhaps the most important secret of Chile is that the top wines from this country cost a fraction of the price of leading wines from other wine regions, and they can deliver outstanding value. One of the reasons for this is that production costs are relatively low.

833. One leading wine from Chile is Seña, which comes from a joint venture between two producers—Mondavi in California and Errazuriz in Chile. The 2003 is a blend of Cabernet Sauvignon, Merlot, Carmenère, and Cabernet Franc. It's a complex swish of dark berries, smoke, vanilla, and anise. It will improve for the next eight years or so in bottle.

834. The best wines of Chile tend to come from higher altitudes, where temperatures fluctuate significantly from day to night. This oscillation helps the grapes develop broad complexity, as well as good levels of acidity to balance the ripe fruit flavors that occur naturally in this hot climate. Alto Maipo is one such region, another is Alto Cachapoal. Alto means high.

835. An outstanding producer in Alto Cachapoal yet to be fully discovered by wine enthusiasts is Altaïr Vineyards and Winery, which is a joint venture between the Chilean producer San Pedro and France's Château Dassault. Altaïr makes just two wines: Altaïr and Sideral.

836. The super-premium wine called Altaïr, with its blend of Cabernet Sauvignon, Carmenère, and Merlot, is a shimmering and intense wine of cassis, black currant, cedar, espresso beans, fleshy plum, and tobacco. The slightly less expensive Sideral wine from the same producer is a wild-eyed yet suave animal of fruit, smoke, and spice made with a blend of Cabernet Sauvignon, Merlot, Syrah, and Sangiovese. Both are amazing wines that have only been around since 2002.

837. The Marnier Lapostolle family of France partnered with the Rabat family of Chile to form Casa Lapostolle, a winery in Chile that makes very good wines. It produces Clos Apalta, one the best wines coming from that long narrow strip of a country today. Clos Apalta is a rugged earthy wine with ferocious fruit and thrusting depth. First produced in 1997, Clos Apalta is made in limited quantities and blends Merlot, Carmenère, and Cabernet Sauvignon.

838. Casa Lapostolle launched a super-premium wine in May 2006 called BOROBO. This first release is a blend of Bordeaux, Rhône, and Burgundy grape varieties from the 2002 vintage, and takes its name from these famous French regions ('BO' from Bordeaux, 'RO' from Rhône, and 'BO' from Bourgogne). BOROBO 2002 is 35 percent Syrah, 20 percent Cabernet Sauvignon, 20 percent Carmenère, 15 percent Pinot Noir, and 10 percent Merlot, reflecting the grapes of the famous French regions.

839. Other top wines from Chile include Don Max and Viñedo Chadwick—both by Errazuriz Wines. These are to Chile, what Premier Crus are to Bordeaux, France—at a snip of the price.

840. The Maipo region of Chile produces some of the best Cabernet Sauvignons in the country. It's the word to watch for on labels when reaching for this variety.

841. Escudo Rojo is a stunning wine from Chile's Maipo region made by Baron Philippe de Rothchild SA, the Bordeaux-based producer. Escudo Rojo blends Cabernet Sauvignon and Merlot to create a dark and intense wine with aromas of violet, ripe, juicy plums, black cherries, cedar, as well as subtle smoke, spice, and vanilla. The silky mouthfeel enrobes the palate with chocolate and mocha. At under $20, it's a steal.

842. Casablanca is a region renowned for its Sauvignon Blanc and Chardonnay wines. Look for Casablanca on a label when shopping for a crisp Chilean white.

843. Carmenère is Chile's most distinctive grape variety. Cuttings of Carmenère arrived from Bordeaux in the late nineteenth century and for years growers confused it with Merlot. Carmenère can produce a luscious, spicy wine of deep and alluring color. Casillero Del Diablo makes a good version that tastes of plums, chocolate, coffee, and toasty oak—unbeatable for under $10.

844. Syrah is making headway in Chile with different styles, depending on where it is grown. Syrah from the Rapel, Maipo, and Aconcagua regions yield full, berry-rich wines from fruit swollen to maximum ripeness in the hot sun. Meanwhile, Syrah from the cooler Chilean areas of Elqui, Limarí, and Casablanca are elegant, savory, meaty expressions of the land and grape.

845. Cousino Macul makes an affordable Cabernet Sauvignon that offers compelling value for the money. The 2002 is well-balanced with flavors of berries and nuts.

846. Errazuriz, Cono Sur, Casa Lapostolle, and Concha y Toro are four reliable producers making wines of consistent quality.

847. The first vines were planted in Chile in 1551 and the resulting wine was used for sacramental purposes by the devout Catholic Spanish settlers.

848. Organic viticulture is easy to practice in Chile thanks to its climate and geography. Many wines are now officially organic and some producers are pursuing biodynamic viticulture.

849. Carmen produces top-notch organic wines under its Nativa label. It is Chile's oldest wine brand, established in 1850.

850. The vineyard that produces Seña is going biodynamic in the near future to capture the best expression of the terroir.

851. Best recent vintages for Chile include 1999, 2000, 2003, and 2004.

21

Argentinean Wine

852. The flagship red grape of Argentina is Malbec, the same variety that's used to make the blockbuster reds of Cahors in France and season Bordeaux blends for spice and clout. Argentina's Malbec wines are riper and softer than their French counterparts.

853. The Mendoza region of Argentina is known for its ability to create splendid Malbec wine. Look for Malbec and Mendoza together on the label.

854. Although Argentina grows and sells the usual varieties, such as Chardonnay, Sauvignon Blanc, and Chenin Blanc, the native Torrontés is worth trying. It is the country's most important quality white grape variety and makes a fleshy, floral wine with hints of peach.

855. Like many other New World countries, you can count on grape varieties to appear on labels of wine from Argentina.

856. Argentina makes wines similar to those of Australia at the lower price points. Both countries produce fruit-forward, full-bodied, approachable wines meant to be drank young.

857. The country has not yet fully recovered from the major economic crash of 2001–2002 so Argentina is desperate to export its wines. This fact, combined with the low relative value of the country's currency, means Argentinean wines can offer very convincing value for the money.

858. Cooler patches in the Andes Mountains produce the most elegant and refined wines with considerable complexity. One such wine, which is a Bordeaux look-alike, is Cheval des Andes. This wine is the product of a joint venture between Terrazas de los Andes in Argentina and Château Cheval-Blanc in Bordeaux, France. Cheval des Andes blends Cabernet Sauvignon, Malbec, and Petit Verdot, to create deeply expressive flavors of macerated berries, cigar box aromas, and dark bitter chocolate. The first vintage available in North America was 2001.

859. A new wine from Argentina that's worth looking for is A Crux by O. Fournier. It's an unfiltered red and its first vintage, 2001, is mainly Tempranillo. It is a rich, earthy wine with tobacco and black stone fruit flavors. The 2002, which is mainly Malbec, shows spiced dark berries, dried herbs, and black truffle, but will become increasingly complex with age.

860. Top Argentinean producers today include Alta Vista, Altos Los Hormigas, Ben Marco, Bodegas Salentein, Catena Zapata, Clos de los Siete, Norton, and Finca la Celia.

861. Mendoza has enjoyed a streak of good vintages from 2002 through 2005.

862. Good recent vintages for Argentina generally include 1999, 2003, and 2004.

22.

Australian Wine

863. Australian wine is sunshine in a glass. It generally delivers an ultraripe style of wine that's extreme: heavily fruit laden, loud in extract, potent in alcohol, dark in color, and deeply aromatic—not surprising given the climate. Australian wine is very popular, particularly in the United Kingdom, United States, New Zealand, Canada, and Germany—the five countries that import the majority of Australian wine.

864. Although Australia commands a lot of shelf space in major export markets, it's actually the seventh largest wine producing country by volume after France, Italy, Spain, the United States, Argentina, and China.

865. Australian wine has become hugely successful because the bulk of it names the grape variety on the label, offers loads of clean fruit flavor, and is generally quite well-priced. Critics argue the wine is unsubtle, unchallenging, and overripe, but Australia is more than this when you look to top wines by this country's better producers.

866. Wolf Blass Platinum Label Barossa Shiraz 2002 is a fine example of what this island can do. This wine combines subtle layers of black fruit, chocolate, and smoky flavors, as well as fine, ripe tannins and vanilla-spice oak beautifully integrated into the palate. It is built to last.

867. Wolf Blass Yellow Label Cabernet Sauvignon is one of the bestselling Australian red wines in North America. Not surprising, really. It consistently provides easy pleasure with ripe tannins, perfect balance, and openhanded amounts of black currant, cassis, vanilla, spice, and mint in the glass, and a long finish after the swallow.

868. Last year, Australian [yellowtail] was the top-selling wine brand in the U.S. The [yellowtail] range is comprised of eleven varietal-labeled bottles that cost about $6 and five single-variety reserve wines that cost about $9. Some of them are persuasive value for the money—particularly the Merlot, Chardonnay, Cabernet-Merlot, and Cabernet Sauvignon. This may surprise you, but the wines are actually not dry—the sugar is disguised by bold fruit and balancing acidity—yet another case of wine drinkers thinking dry and drinking sweet.

869. [yellowtail] Chardonnay 2005 starts with the perfume of sun-ripened oranges and lemons and carries through with zesty flavors of bright, fleshy citrus fruit, and then finishes with vanilla and coconut.

870. [yellowtail] Merlot 2005 is pure cherry-vanilla with a creamy mouthfeel.

871. [yellowtail] Cabernet Merlot 2004 layers cherry-vanilla with clean cassis flavor and gentle tannins.

872. [yellowtail] Cabernet Sauvignon 2005 is perhaps the best value of all with rich blackberry liqueur, leather, and enough concentration and length to deliver considerable value.

873. Yalumba, Australia's oldest family-owned winery, crafts a range of wines labeled Oxford Landing. These wines cost about $6 and are excellent expressions of the grape variety noted on each bottle. Pure clean fruit, excellent balance, good weight, and always a pleasure to drink if you're looking for a straightforward drink at a low price.

874. Yalumba's Y Series wines are a step up from the Oxford Landing range and offer shining examples of pure fruit expression, labeled with their grape variety. The Viognier in this range is particularly good. Vintage after vintage, this wine displays honeysuckle and flowers, citrus and spice, and a satiny smooth mouthfeel.

875. Gemtree makes a beautiful premium wine called Uncut Shiraz from McLaren Vale. The 2002 is intense and spicy with deep, dark, concentrated fruit laced with pumpkin spice aromas.

876. Petaluma Chardonnay is a wine I turn to for one big swirl of nectarine, almonds, and creamy vanilla. It's a particularly silky rendition of this grape.

877. Barossa Valley is perhaps the best area in Australia for producing world-class Shiraz. Penfolds Grange, which is Australia's top super-premium red wine, originally sourced its Shiraz grapes from the Barossa Valley.

878. Penfolds Grange is not only Australia's most famous red wine, it's one of the country's very finest. Its first vintage was in 1951 and since then it has gained cult status with a ripe, fruit-forward style of oaked Shiraz showing minimal vintage variation. It sells for about $200 per bottle and requires cellaring for at least ten years to develop its potential. The hallmark flavors are dark chocolate, vanilla bean, black licorice, spice, black pepper, mixed forest fruit, smoke, and tobacco.

879. Penfolds is a reliable producer of a huge range of wines. Its Bin 28 Kalimna Shiraz is a very credible value. Dense black cherry flavors, smoky notes, and a round, smooth mouthfeel pack this wine with a hefty dose of pleasure.

880. Penfolds Koonunga Hill range provides good value for the money—the perfect fit for a backyard barbecue. The Koonunga Hill Shiraz Cabernet is an inexpensive yet warm and inviting wine of considerable charm. Tightly wound and well-balanced, it exudes aromas and flavors of black currant and rhubarb, olive and chocolate, smoked meat and wood, licorice and spice—a lot of complexity for less than $10.

881. Many lower-end oaked wines from Australia are made by adding wood staves or bags of oak chips to wine fermenting in steel tanks as an inexpensive alternative to barrel-aging. This keeps the price per bottle down since barrels are expensive, but it can produce a style where the wood flavors are less integrated. Slapstick oak.

882. Amberley, a producer in Margaret River, makes quite elegant red wines. The 2003 Cabernet Merlot shows equal parts ripe berries and savory, gamey flavors. Interesting stuff.

883. Australia isn't known for its Pinot Noir, but Nepenthe Wines makes a version that lovers of this variety should consider tasting. Nepenthe's Charleston Pinot Noir 2003 is all dried herbs, black cherries, farmyard, and earth and yields a long, lingering finish.

884. Australia makes a number of dessert wines and one of the best is Angove's Anchorage Old Tawny, made in the style of a Tawny Port. The depth of flavor and complexity is very impressive and, if tasted blind, could be mistaken for a high-quality Tawny Port. It tastes of dried fruit, honey, butterscotch, and the best fruitcake you've ever eaten.

885. Some of the leading producers in Australia are Brokenwood, Brown Brothers, Cullen Wines, Gemtree, Hardy's, Henschke, Penfolds, Petaluma, Peter Lehmann, Turkey Flat, Tyrrell's, Wirra Wirra Vineyards, Wolf Blass, Mitchelton Wines, Wynn's Coonawarra Estate, and Yalumba.

886. Two fine organic producers are Jasper Hill Winery and Cullen Wines.

887. A notable biodynamic producer in Australia is Castagna Vineyard.

888. Best recent vintages in Australia include 2001, 2003, and 2004.

23.

New Zealand Wine

889. Marlborough makes a unique style of Sauvignon Blanc that is very ripe, very crisp, and tastes like gooseberries. Marlborough Sauvignon Blanc took the world by storm in the 1980s and planted New Zealand squarely on the proverbial winemaking map.

890. Cloudy Bay is the most popular Sauvignon Blanc from Marlborough. It was the first to be seriously exported in the mid '80s and quickly garnered rave reviews by critics. It now enjoys cult status and is a cracking version of this grape. It's also now owned by the luxury goods conglomerate LVMH.

891. Since Cloudy Bay, dozens of Marlborough producers began exporting their Sauvignon Blanc and they all taste very similar unless sampled side by side. The secret here is, if you like Cloudy Bay, you can get a comparable wine for less by looking for other Sauvignon Blanc wines from lesser known Marlborough producers. I particularly like the one by Villa Maria.

892. Sacred Hill does some beautiful things with Sauvignon Blanc under the label Sauvage. Barrel fermentation plus twelve months aging in oak gives the wine a toasty, nutty flavor beneath layers of restrained gooseberry, orange, pineapple, and lemon-lime. There are also warm butterscotch flavors on the finish. Winning wine. Reliable producer.

893. Although New Zealand Pinot Noir is regarded as the next big grape variety coming out of the country, buy it with caution. Quality is still spotty.

894. If you're looking to see what New Zealand can do with Pinot Noir, pick up a bottle of Mount Riley's version from 2004. This wine is fairly Burgundian in style, with restrained aromas of caramelized meat drippings and raspberry on the nose, leading to plum, spice, and ripe raspberry on the palate.

895. Felton Road produces a very good Pinot Noir and the 2004 is an exciting mix of smoldering dark fruit, earthy spices, and ripe plum and cherry.

896. If choosing between Oregon and New Zealand Pinot Noir—the two New World leaders in that variety right now—choose Oregon.

897. Villa Maria, Mud House Wines, Sacred Hill, and Trinity Hill are all reliable New Zealand producers.

898. New Zealand is making some very interesting sweet wines. A favorite of mine is the Winemaker's Collection Late Harvest 2001 Riesling by Seifried. It's a sumptuous mix of vanilla, cherries, lime, honey, and marmalade.

899. Milton Winery is a biodynamic producer.

900. Best recent vintages include 2000, 2001, and 2003.

24.

South African Wine

901. The first South African vineyard was planted in 1655 in the Cape, and in 1659 the first wine was made—a modest 15 liters from Muscadel grapes. In 2005, South Africa produced 593.1 million liters of wine.

902. Fairview Estate is one of my favorite South African wine producers. It offers consistent quality across the board. Fairview Estate's Goats do Roam Red, a name that sounds a lot like Côtes du Rhône and thus ruffled French feathers, could easily sell for twice its price. It's a juicy, ripe wine of weight and substance, berries and spice. Fairview Estates is both a cheese producing goat farm and a winery.

903. If you come across a wine called Oom Pagel from Fairview Estate, snap it up. It's a white wine made from Sémillon and tastes of citrus, cream, and almonds with a round, full mouthfeel and a lovely lingering finish. Lovable, fleshy sort of wine that you would want to curl up with after a hard day at work.

904. Pinotage is South Africa's flagship grape, and has a very distinct flavor of black licorice. It was created in 1925 when the Pinot Noir grape was successfully cross-pollinated with Cinsault.

905. Though Pinotage has long been recognized as South Africa's most distinctive red grape, South Africa is producing outstanding wines from Merlot, Cabernet Sauvignon, Grenache, and especially Shiraz/Syrah.

906. Kumala makes a good Cabernet Sauvignon that costs less than $10. The 2004 packs blackberry, black currant, pepper, and subtle puffs of warm smoke. Very well-balanced and deserving of every dollar spent.

907. Garagiste winemaker Tom Lubbe creates very small amounts of highly acclaimed Syrah, called The Observatory. He uses grapes from his own farm in the mountainous Paardeberg area northwest of Cape Town. Then, he makes the wine in a small converted shed.

908. Chenin Blanc is traditionally South Africa's best white, and it can age well. Morgenhof produces an outstanding one from vines more than thirty years old. The 2004 is scrumptious showing flowers and stones, lemon, and herbs, and spice and butter with good length. This Chenin Blanc will develop nicely in the bottle until about 2008 and keep longer.

909. The country is producing some excellent Sauvignon Blanc, Chardonnay, and Sémillon. In fact, South Africa is one of the world's most exciting Sauvignon Blanc producers today. Look for those from Neil Ellis and Jordan Winery.

910. Neil Ellis Sauvignon Blanc 2005 is a pale, glossy wine with pure asparagus aromas wafting from the glass. It leads to an asparagus, lemon, and gooseberry palate. Reliable value and a delight with grilled prawns.

911. The Jordan Winery is known as Jardin Winery in the United States to avoid the conflict with the Californian winery of the same name. Jordan/Jardin's 2004 Sauvignon Blanc is an expressive, complex wine of herbs, smoked pear, grass, asparagus, lemon, and wet stones.

912. Kuwala Chardonnay 2004 from the Western Cape of South Africa demonstrates South Africa's ability to make very good value wines under $10. This wine is a polished gem of a wine with clear fruit definition—oranges and apricot nose and palate—and a flair that's rarely found in New World wines at this price.

913. The 2003 Neil Ellis Chardonnay is a Burgundian style white of very high caliber. Think melon, cool stones, and hints of buttered toast and oak.

914. Méthode Cap Classique is South Africa's name for making sparkling wine. It involves creating a second fermentation in bottle.

915. Graham Beck produces a good sparkling wine simply called Graham Beck Brut Rosé. It's made from the same grapes as Champagne—Pinot Noir and Chardonnay—but is a fruity, full style with bright berry aromas and flavors. Much less restrained than Champagne.

916. Wines from South Africa bearing a vintage date must be made of at least 75 percent of grapes from that year, and those noting a grape variety on the label must contain at least 85 percent of that type of fruit.

917. Jordan Vineyards, Springfield Estate, and Boekenhoutskloof are excellent wine producers in South Africa.

918. Rozendal Farm practices organic viti-culture and the vineyards are transitioning to biodynamic methods.

919. Reyneke Wines is a biodynamic producer.

920. Vintages 2001 through 2004 have all been very good in South Africa.

25.

Wine from the Rest of the World

921. Château Indage and Grover Vineyards produce the best wines coming out of India today.

922. China and Japan produce wine, but it's nothing to write home about—yet. Ironically, China made the world's first wine about nine thousand years ago, which was made from rice.

923. England and Wales have started producing some very good dry white wine, especially those made from the hearty Müller-Thurgau and Seyval Blanc grapes that can withstand the cool climates and lack of sunshine. These wines tend to be very crisp and refreshing. Good summertime options.

924. Brazil and Uruguay are two countries in South America, other than Chile and Argentina, that make some promising wine.

925. Generally, commercial vineyards are only viable between two bands of latitude—30–50° north and 30–50° south of the equator. Outside of these broad strips, it's difficult to make wine of any real quality. For that reason, not all countries make wine.

926. Global warming is slowly changing the climates of every country. In time, more regions of the world will be able to make wine; places that are too cold to make anything but white and sparkling wines will be able to grow red grapes, too; and tasting profiles of classic wines will shift.

Part Four:

Trade Secrets

One of the best things about working in wine is the bits of useful information you glean that heighten your appreciation and understanding of the drink. This part of the book gathers these bits and bobs, and spills them across the page: wine myths that you and I have probably heard a hundred times but are dead wrong; correct and incorrect ways to store your stash; tips on giving wine since this small act can be so much more interesting than just handing someone a bottle; and which sources are most reliable when you want to know more. To complete your little bundle of 1,000 secrets, I've tacked on a lexicon of the most practical wine terms. But first, the myths...

Part Four

Trade Secrets

26.

Wine Myths

927. Myth: You should uncork a bottle of wine to let it breathe a little before pouring it. Truth: Merely uncorking a bottle of wine only exposes the surface of the liquid in the bottle neck to air, so the amount of aeration is minimal. This will have no perceivable effect on the wine. Instead, decant it to aerate it.

928. Myth: The finer the bubbles, the better the bubbly. Truth: Bubble size has no bearing on the quality of Champagne nor any other sparkling wine. Much research has been done on the subject recently, particularly by Gérard Liger-Belair, associate professor of physical sciences at the University of Reims Champagne-Ardenne in the heart of the Champagne region. Turns out, the temperature of the wine, as well as the size of the impurities and faults on the inside of the wine glass, all affect the size of the bubbles. The warmer the Champagne, the larger and more frequent the bubbles. And without faults or impurities on the glass, such as microscopic streaks left by a dishtowel, Champagne looks like perfectly still white wine that, when drank, feels fizzy.

929. Myth: Drink red wine with cheese and meat, and whites with fish and poultry. Truth: There are many exceptions to this overused rule. Fuller-bodied white wines as well as sweet ones can be delicious with cheese. Red wine from Pinot Noir grapes can be excellent with turkey. And a light-bodied red such as Beaujolais or another well-made Gamay goes very well with chicken.

930. Myth: Gewürztraminer and Asian foods are a perfect match. Truth: This aromatic, full-bodied wine would overpower any of the mild cornerstones of Asian cuisine such as dim sum, tempura, or sashimi. Plus, Gewürztraminer is notoriously lacking in acidity, which is the cleansing agent in wine needed to refresh the palate for many of the other staples of Asian cuisine—fried tempura, oily duck, or fatty tuna belly known as toro fish.

931. Myth: Vintage charts dictate good and bad wines. Truth: Completely good and bad vintages don't exist. Wine regions typically charted in vintage guides are huge geographic areas where weather varies so some producers experience great conditions in so-called poor vintages. Also, a highly acclaimed vintage is no guarantee of quality because grape growing and winemaking practices influence the quality of the wine as much as weather does. Use vintage charts as a general guide only, if at all.

932. Myth: If it's popular, it must be good. Truth: Just because it sells well doesn't mean it's delicious. A prime example is Pinot Grigio. In 2003, Pinot Grigio was the bestselling imported white wine in the U.S., according to the trade publication *Impact Databank*. Yet, at best, it's merely inoffensive and bland. Pinot Grigio tastes vaguely of citrus. It's a light, neutral wine. Perhaps the collective North American palate got so weary of big, heavy, oaked Chardonnay, that Pinot Grigio refreshed tired palates with its light, clean style. For a similarly crisp, clean style, look to Chablis or Muscadet from France; Müller-Thurgau from Austria, Britain, or Canada; or Silvaner from Germany, all of which offer a little more flavor and all the freshness.

933. Myth: You only decant red wine. Truth: Many white wines of distinction, such as Sauternes, or white Burgundies from better properties also benefit from decanting because the aeration brings out their aromas and flavors.

934. Myth: Champagne doesn't age well. Truth: Good quality Champagne ages extremely well. One of the most mesmerizing wines I've ever tasted was a 1970 Cristal, courtesy of Champagne Louis Roederer. Unforgettable. Tasted when it was thirty-two years old in London, England, the wine was a charming kiss of brioche and cooked apple with layers of nuts, fresh bread, crème caramel, lacy acidity, and a long, lively finish. Sublime.

935. Myth: Blended wine is poor quality. Truth: Though sometimes a wine from one type of grape can be very good, blending two or more varieties can produce better balance, complexity, and harmony. In fact, wine laws in most places allow wines labeled as a single grape variety to be seasoned with other types of grapes to let winemakers blend for balance.

936. Myth: The Old World makes better wine than the New World. Truth: Both the Old and New Worlds make good and bad wines and although they traditionally made very different styles of wine, overlap is starting to occur. Buying the best wine comes down to understanding your personal taste, choosing wine styles that appeal to you, and buying wines from trusted, quality-minded producers.

937. Myth: Red grapes always make red wine and white ones always make white. Truth: Although this is usually the case, red grapes can make white wine. Such is the case with Champagne. The three grapes that go into this white sparkler include Chardonnay, which is of course white, as well as Pinot Noir and Pinot Meunier—two red grapes. Gentle pressing keeps the red grape skins from imparting color to the wine.

938. Myth: Old wines taste better than young ones. Truth: This is seldom true because the vast majority of wine made today is released from the winery at its peak and ready to drink. If these ready-to-drink wines are aged, they will be older but not better because they're not made to bear the weight of time. Wines designed for cellaring are the only ones that actually improve with age. Chapter 4 reveals the secrets of knowing when to drink a wine.

27.

Storing Wine

939. A stable, cool temperature between 40°F and 59°F is ideal for storing wine and the temperature shouldn't fluctuate by more than about 12 degrees. Why? Because a rise in temperature can cause the bubble of air between the cork and the wine to expand, forcing wine out between the cork and the bottle. Then, a temperature drop can create a vacuum, forcing oxygen in through the cork. And of course, oxygen is wine's greatest enemy. For this reason, be careful when transporting good bottles of wine when it's very hot or cold outside.

940. Despite the secret above, good wine can generally withstand the odd temperature fluctuation. The cellars of Bordeaux in France for instance fluctuate by a few degrees seasonally, which doesn't hurt the wines. The reason is probably the gradual rate at which the temperatures change.

941. You also want to store wine in a fairly humid environment if you're laying them down for any length of time. Humidity levels over 50 percent ensure wine corks don't dry out and shrink, which can let oxygen in and wine out.

942. To be sure your best bottles remain in fine form, you can invest in a temperature and humidity controlled storage cabinet—Eurocave is the current leading producer. Another option is to buy a cooling and humidifying unit for your insulated cellar.

943. If you choose to trust the conditions of that little room in your basement for aging your best bottles, invest in a digital thermo-hygrometer. It's a device that costs about $50 at your hardware store and tracks the humidity and temperature of the space, including the minimum and maximum levels. Placing a basin of water in the room can improve humidity levels in a pinch.

944. If a wine is sealed with a screwcap or plastic cork-like plug, it's generally not made for aging, so drink it as young as possible.

945. As a wine matures in bottle, chemical reactions happen that change the wine. Storage time changes the balance of fruit, alcohol, tannin, and acidity; increases the complexity of flavors and aromas; and eventually makes it unpleasant to drink. A rise in temperature speeds up these chemical reactions so a warm storage spot for your wine will age it faster. This means, don't store bottles you want to keep fresh—like that delicate Loire white or Beaujolais Nouveau—in warm places, such as in the cupboard over the stove. On the other hand, if your cellar is very cold, your ageworthy wines might last longer than you think.

946. Store wine bottles on their sides, ideally with the neck sloping slightly upwards. This position keeps the cork wet, the air bubble between the stopper and the wine in the bottle's shoulder, and sediment collecting towards the bottle base.

947. Ever wonder why some better Champagnes are wrapped in curiously heavy cellophane? It's because the wrap is actually light-proof. Light can change the flavor of wines, particularly sparkling ones. Long-term exposure to light can produce flavors of wet cardboard—a condition known as "light struck." This is why wines should be stored in the dark and why many are now sold in very dark bottles. It's also a reason to avoid buying wines that seem to have been sitting in the bright light of a wine merchant's window for ages.

948. Storing wine away from major vibrations is a good idea as not to disturb the wine's intricate chemical alchemy while aging. If good wine has been subjected to vibrations, let it rest a few weeks before serving.

949. Make sure wine is stored away from harsh smells, such as paint and household cleaners. Wines can take on these smells.

950. Exposure to air changes the flavors of a wine by oxidizing it. If you open a bottle for only a glass or two, an easy method of preserving the remaining wine is to transfer it into a clean, empty half bottle because it exposes less of the wine to air. A bottle of wine will last a few extra days this way, gradually losing its finesse.

951. If you hire a company specializing in wine storage to take care of your bottles for you, make sure the organization is fully licensed and has a good track record.

28.

Giving the Gift of Wine

952. If you're bringing wine to a dinner party as a hostess gift, don't assume it will be served with the meal. The host or hostess has probably chosen a wine for that purpose.

953. If you bring a wine to a party that you're eager to try, tell the host or hostess you're keen to "taste" it. Or else, bring it decanted.

954. In Britain, they sometimes give wine to celebrate the birth of a baby. The idea is to give the baby wine from the vintage of his or her birth year that will improve with long-term aging. Top quality Bordeaux is particularly ideal for this purpose because it's made to last. In a good year, some such bottles will continue to improve and keep for fifty years or more, which would mean the recipient would be able to enjoy the wine at some of his or her life's milestone occasions.

955. An excellent hostess gift is a small bottle of fine Champagne. Too few people buy this sort of thing for themselves and it's always a joy to receive.

956. The gift of wine doesn't have to come bottled. A ticket to a wine-maker's dinner is an exciting way to be introduced to new wines, and these events happen more often than you may think. A good source of tasting events throughout the world can be found at www.localwineevents.com.

957. Certain bottles of bubbly are always excellent gifts because of their obvious quality—Champagne by Louis Roederer, Krug, or Bollinger come to mind—but they do tend to be big ticket items.

958. If you have a wine enthusiast on your Christmas list, give a membership to a wine club, such as the The Wine Society or the Opimian Society, or a subscription to a wine magazine such as *Decanter*.

29.

Learning More about Wine

959. The bible of wine information is *The Oxford Companion to Wine* by Jancis Robinson. Jancis is a Master of Wine and widely regarded as a leading authority on all things wine. She writes a regular column for the *Financial Times* newspaper in London, England.

960. The Wine & Spirit Education Trust offers some of the best wine courses in the world, which are now available in twenty-eight countries and eight languages.

961. To keep abreast of best buys and producers, subscribe to *Decanter* magazine. As far as I am concerned, it is the best wine magazine on the market. For up-to-the-minute wine news, visit www.decanter.com.

962. Starting a wine-tasting group with friends is a great way to try wines affordably and learn about different styles. Pool funds, buy some wines, and share thoughts on very good bottles. Then, pull straws to take home the remains.

963. Joining a wine club is a way to band together with other enthusiasts to buy wine, learn more about the topic, and attend tastings. Major wine clubs include the Opimian Society in Canada, The Wine Society in the UK, and The American Wine Society in the U.S.

964. Most great wine regions have routes to follow that will take you cellar to cellar. I can't think of a better way to learn about wine.

965. Tim Atkin's wine column in *The Observer* newspaper in London is one of the best. He not only knows wine inside and out from years of experience and expertise as a Master of Wine, but his writing is witty, accessible, and frank. Always a pleasure to read.

966. Don't just read about it, drink it.

967. Keep a wine journal and record your thoughts on every wine you taste—even if it's just a few words. Track those that impress you.

968. Andrew Jefford's writing on wine is among the most eloquent. He writes a regular column for *Decanter* magazine that's usually infused with poetic prose and a philosophical slant. He has written a number of books including *The New France*, which has won two major literary awards so far.

969. *Gambero Rosso* is the world's leading guide to Italian wines, and is available in English and Italian.

970. France's top wine guide is *Classement des Meilleurs Vins de France*. It is published annually.

971. The most influential critic in the United States is Robert Parker. He issues a bimonthly newsletter called *The Wine Advocate* to more than 45,000 subscribers in thirty-eight countries, and has penned a dozen books. Robert Parker's palate seems to favor wines that are concentrated and fruit-driven. This style tends to also be favored by much of the North American market, which probably contributes to his success.

972. Hugh Johnson is perhaps the most influential wine critic in the UK. His *Pocket Wine Guide* alone has sold over seven million copies, and has been printed in twelve languages. He also contributes a regular column in *Decanter* magazine. His taste in wine is probably the polar opposite to that of Robert Parker. He prefers elegance and restraint to power and fruit-laden styles—preferences that arguably mirror the British collective palate.

973. Buying wine from a knowledgeable merchant is a great way to learn more about wine. Here are some secrets about fine wine merchants:

- If you happen to travel to London, England, consider visiting the independent wine merchant, Lea & Sandeman. Charles Lea is a top-notch expert on Burgundy, and Patrick Sandeman is an authority on Italy. Each has excellent insight into these fragmented and confusing regions. Both gentlemen work out of the shop's Chelsea location at 170 Fulham Road.
- Zachys, the U.S. fine wine merchant in Scarsdale, New York, offers a terrific selection of wines, particularly from Bordeaux, Burgundy, Italy, and Spain. They also have an online store at www.zachys.com.
- Best Cellars is a chain of wine merchants in the U.S. that categorizes its wares by taste—fizzy, fresh, soft, luscious, juicy, smooth, etc. Most wines are under $15. Check them out at www.bestcellars.com.

- If you live in Ontario, Canada, where the sale of alcoholic beverages is controlled by a government monopoly, you still have the option of buying wine from a knowledgeable wine merchant. The Liquor Control Board of Ontario (LCBO) licenses agencies who sell directly to consumers as well as restaurants. You may have to wait a few months to receive the wine and you're required to buy it by the case, but the odds of buying good quality wines when you buy through an agent are stacked in your favor because they can provide you with good counsel. Look to the Ontario Imported Wine-Spirit-Beer Association (www.oiwsba.com) for a list of licensed agents.

- Ne Plus Ultra Agencies in Toronto offers a good selection of Portuguese and Spanish wines. It's a small operation run by a couple of experts in the Iberian Peninsula. They don't have a web presence but their telephone number is 416-964-8180. Two other top-notch agencies in Canada are Lifford Wine Agency—www.liffordwineagency.com—and Churchill Cellars Ltd.—www.churchillcellars.com.

30.

Talking the Talk—Wine Terminology

974. Anthocyanin: The pigments just under grape skins, which color wine. Recent studies show anthocyanins, along with other naturally occurring substances in red wine, are very healthy and may prevent a number of human diseases.

975. Attack: A tasting term that refers to the initial flavor of the wine when it hits the palate.

976. Barrel toast: The process of heating the wood of an oak barrel that will be used for fermenting or aging wine. This heating is done to a winemaker's specifications and the degree of toasting affects the flavor and structure of the wine. Lightly toasted oak imparts tannin from the wood to the wine, but relatively little color and flavor. Heavily toasted oak adds less tannin, more color, and more pronounced flavors of spice, smoke, and often roasted coffee.

977. Biodynamic viticulture: A method of grape growing that is an offshoot of biodynamic agriculture founded by the Austrian mystic Rudolf Steiner in the 1920s. Biodynamic farming, like organic methods, rejects pesticide use to minimize damage to ecosystems. However, while organic farmers add heaps of manure to soil, biodynamic growers only add a teaspoon or so, believing it's enough to harness natural forces streaming in from the cosmos. Biodynamism is rooted firmly in faith.

978. Collar: The bubble ring at the periphery of a glass of sparkling wine.

979. Crémant: Sparkling wine from areas in France other than Champagne. This wine is made fizzy by the traditional method of creating a second fermentation in the bottle.

980. Flabby: A tasting term that means the wine tastes flat due to a lack of acidity or sourness relative to the fruit intensity.

981. Garagiste: Originally a French term for winemakers who produce small quantities of wine from their garages in Bordeaux. Jean-Luc Thunevin was the first garagiste in St. Emilion, Bordeaux, taking the world by storm by producing amazing wines under the label Valandraud. The first vintage was 1991 and by 1996 the prices had soared to more than those of the top Premier Grand Cru Classé wines of the region. Like all fads, the market for these wines deflated, but Thunevin is looking to get his wines recognized formally in 2006 when St. Emilion reclassifies its wines—an event that takes place every ten years. Today, many small-scale wineries all over the world market themselves as garagistes.

982. Green harvesting: When a grower removes bunches of unripe grapes from a vine during the growing season to reduce yields and improve the quality of the remaining clusters.

983. La lutte raisonnée: A method of viticulture adopted by a growing number of French producers that keeps the use of artificial fertilizers, pesticides, herbicides, insecticides, and fungicides to a bare minimum.

984. Lean: A wine with light to medium body and high levels of acidity.

985. Malolactic fermentation: A winemaking process whereby the sour malic acids of a wine are changed to the milder lactic acids to produce better balance. Malic acids are what give green apples their characteristic punch, and lactic acid is the much gentler form found in milk. Wines that have undergone malolactic fermentation are less sour and often show a buttery aroma.

986. Master of Wine: Affectionately referred to in the trade by its abbreviation MW, this accreditation is internationally recognized as the highest level of educational achievement for the wine industry, and is very difficult to earn. When this book went to print, there were just 251 MWs in the world.

987. Meritage: A wine made in the U.S. or Canada exclusively with Bordeaux grape varieties—Cabernet Sauvignon, Cabernet Franc, Merlot, Malbec, and Petit Verdot for reds and Sémillon, Sauvignon Blanc, and Muscadelle for whites. A wine called Meritage must also be produced in fairly small quantities (not exceeding 25,000 cases) and be one of the two most expensive wines a winery produces.

988. Must: Grape juice before it is fermented into wine.

989. Négociant: A merchant who buys grapes, grape juice, or wine and makes wine under his or her own name. Louis Jadot, for instance, is a major négociant in Burgundy. Stone Creek is a major négociant in California.

990. Noble rot: When white grapes destined to become sweet wines are affected by Botrytis cinerea. This mold shrivels the grapes and concentrates their sugars. When Botrytis cinerea affects grapes not destined for sweet wine production, the disease is less favorable and called grey rot.

991. Phenolics: Grape constituents that exist mainly in the stems, skin, and seeds that impart flavor, color, and tannins to wines.

992. Second wine: A wine from the lesser quality or younger grapes of a property known for its "grand vin." This phrase is mainly used in Bordeaux, but is batted around elsewhere, too.

993. Skin contact: When white grape skin is left in contact with the pressed juice before fermentation to extract flavor. When red wines are made, grape skins and pulp are left in contact with the juice during and after fermentation to impart color, flavor, and tannin. In red wine, this process is called maceration instead of skin contact.

994. Tannin: A compound found in grape skins, pips, and stems that dissolves in the juice during the red winemaking process, giving red wine an astringent and sometimes bitter quality.

995. Terroir: The French term that means the soil, climate, geography, and geology of an area. Terroir influences the flavors of the grapes and wine from any given place.

996. Veraison: The period in the growing season when the grapes change color.

997. Vinification: Winemaking.

998. Vintage: The year the grapes for a particular wine are harvested.

999. Viticulture: The agricultural act of growing grape vines.

1000. Yeast: The fungus that eats the sugar of grape juice and expels alcohol and carbon dioxide. The resulting liquid is wine.

Appendix A: 50 Best Wines under $20

RED

• La Montesa, 2003, Bodegas Palacios Remondo, Rioja, Spain
Round and plump with fine tannins and good weight. Velvety and lush on the tongue, this wine brims with roasted plum and black cherry flavors mingling with a bit of smoke and spice. It is drinking very well now.

• Moulin-à-Vent Fleur, 2004, Georges Deboeuf, Burgundy, France
Fresh, ripe red berries with hints of flowers and spice. Delicious, refreshing, and versatile. Everything a Beaujolais should be and then some.

• Rasteau, 2003, Perrin & Fils, Côtes du Rhône, France

Ripe raspberries and blueberries dipped in dark chocolate with hints of vanilla and spice on the finish. Wines like this are why the Rhône region has gained such a following.

• Château les Trois Croix, 2002, AC Fronsac, Bordeaux, France

Made from low yielding vines, this tight-knit wine made by the former winemaker of the revered Château Mouton Rothschild brims with rich red and black cherry flavors and hints of warm stones and earth. Ripe, silky tannins wrap the fruit beautifully. Drink now to 2010.

• Coudoulet de Beaucastel, Château de Beaucastel, Côtes du Rhône, France

This wine is consistently delicious vintage after vintage with lots of lush spicy, meaty, fleshy fruit layered with coffee, smoke, leather, and earth.

• Nipozzano, Frescobaldi, 2002, Chianti Rufina Riserva, Italy

Seriously delicious wine with bold fruit, silky tannins, and flavors that flit from cherry to licorice, prunes to spice. A beautiful wine that benefits from a double decant.

- Escudo Rojo, 2002, Baron Philippe de Rothschild, Maipo, Chile

Dark and intense with aromas of violet, ripe plums, black cherries, cedar, as well as subtle smoke, spice, and vanilla. Silky mouthfeel with chocolate and mocha on the finish.

- Campfiorin, 2002, Masi, Veneto, Italy

Rich and beautifully ripe with deep concentration. Will age gracefully until 2009 but drinks well now. Youthful flavors of black cherry and red and black plum with some raisin and spice in the background. Soft, ripe tannins. Medium to long length. Excellent value.

- Cabernet Sauvignon, 2002, Wynn's Coonawarra Estate, Coonawarra, Australia

Spiced stone fruit, warm chocolate, and mellow coffee flavors make this a welcoming wine to come home to.

- Cabernet Sauvignon, 2005, Casillero del Diablo, Concha y Toro, Maipo Valley, Chile

Winemaker Marchelo Papa makes excellent wines with his Casillero del Diablo range, which translates to cellar of the devil. The Cabernet Sauvignon is my favorite, with intense dark berry and plum flavors wrapped with layers of warm vanilla and rich mocha.

• Carménère, 2004, Casillero Del Diablo, Concha y Toro, Maipo Valley, Chile
A stunning version of this grape variety at an unbeatable price of under $10. Plums, chocolate, coffee, toasty oak—and perfect balance.

• Merlot, 2004, Cono Sur, Central Valley, Chile
Adolfo Hurtado, the young winemaker at Cono Sur, delivers charm in a bottle with this well-formed, voluptuous Merlot that resonates with blackberries, plums, and chocolate. Very stylish wine at a great price.

• Reserve Merlot, 2001, Vina Carmen, Rapel Valley, Chile
Lush and spicy nose of thyme, black cherry, white flowers, and lavender lead to flavors of bitter chocolate, black cherry, and pepper. The palate is smooth and ripe with soft tannins, juicy berry fruit, and a lovely depth of flavor.

• Petalos del Bierzo, 2004, Descendientes de Jose Palacios, Bierzo, Spain.
This carefully handmade wine is an intense and serious sipper by one of the most respected wine-makers in Spain, Alvaro Palacios. With meticu-lous attention to detail in the vineyards and the winery, he has made this elegant wine that tastes of red bell pepper, forest fruits, herbs, and spice, and delivers a lengthy finish of black pepper and smoke. As soon as I tasted it, I bought some for my cellar.

• Reserva Alentejo, 2001, Sogrape, Alentejo, Portugal
Creamy hot cocoa, luscious plums, plump raisins, and vanilla.

• Seven Hills Merlot, 2001, L'Ecole No 41, Walla Walla Valley, Washington, USA
Caramelized meat drippings and marzipan on the nose followed by an attack of marzipan, violets, black pepper, smoke, and berries on the palate. Delicious.

• Calvet Reserve Rouge, 2002, Bordeaux, France
Cedar, pencil shavings, black currant, spice, and cherry flavors swishing around this medium-bodied wine that's always reliable almost regardless of vintage.

• Koonunga Hill Shiraz Cabernet, Barossa, McLaren Vale and Coonawarra, Australia
I can't improve on the chief winemaker's notes, which describe the wine as spicy with aromas and flavors of dark fruit, quince, fig, hints of olive and licorice, smoky meats, dark chocolate, and fruitcake.

• Red Reserva, 2000, Marqués de Riscal, Rioja, Spain
Cinnamon and spice, blueberries and raspberries, smoke and milk chocolate, and hints of caramel and vanilla. Look for the bottle enmeshed in gold thread and bearing a white and gold label.

• Bin 28 Shiraz, 2001, Penfolds, South Australia
Smooth and full of fruit with a round, easy-to-drink-quality. Concentrated black cherry flavors with smoky notes. Excellent balance and value.

• Shiraz Show Reserve, 1998, Wyndham Estate, Hunter Valley, Australia
Interesting flavors of caramelized pan drippings, leather, and raspberries, with hints of dark chocolate and tobacco. Long peppery, robust finish. Drinking very well now. Well-balanced. Excellent choice for a prime joint of roasted meat.

• Zinfandel Vintners Blend, 2003, Ravenswood, California, USA
Joel Peterson is the winemaker behind this wine that delivers incredible value for about $10. He makes a variety of other single vineyard Zinfandels, but I like this one best. It is all about clean ripe blueberries and blackberries, ultraripe raspberries, warm spice, and supple tannins. It's the perfect thing to bring to a barbecue.

• Tatone Montepulciano d'Abuzzo, 2000, Terra d'Aligi, Abruzzo, Italy
Deep, almost opaque wine with clean aromas of blackberry, blueberry, cherry, and spearmint. A smooth, rich palate of concentrated berry flavors fills the mouth, along with nuances of dark chocolate, tobacco, and black pepper. This wine is drinking well now but will continue to develop for at least five years. Drink it in the fall or winter with roasted beef.

- Artist Series Cabernet Sauvignon, 2001, Woodward Canyon, Washington State, USA
This wine exudes curious aromas of barbecued steak and black peppercorns followed by flavors of charred beef and red plums. A bit of mineral and green pepper on the finish.

- Yellow Label Cabernet Sauvignon, 2002, Wolf Blass, South Australia
This wine gives easy pleasure with cleansingly bright acidity, ripe tannins, and perfect balance, as well as vanilla, spice, cassis, mint, and a long finish after the swallow.

- Merlot, 2002, Pikes, Clare Valley, Australia
Black forest cake in a glass—sour cherry, dark chocolate, a rich creamy mouthfeel, and complete satisfaction.

- Castillo de Almansa Tinto Reserva, 2001, Bodegas Piqueras, Almansa, Spain
Tremendous value for the money. All fresh berries, leather, dried fruit, and spice.

- Castillo Ygay Tinto Gran Reserva, 2001, Bodegas Marqués de Murrieta, Rioja, Spain
Toasted oak, black and red berries, and spice. This wine is intense and meaty, yet exquisitely polished. Long and drinking beautifully.

WHITE

• Sauvignon Blanc, 2003, Robertson Winery, Breede River, South Africa
Grapefruit aromas laced with whiffs of smoke and stone lead to grapefruit, tangerine, mineral, and herbs on the palate with a green pepper finish. This is a restrained style of Sauvignon Blanc.

• Marlborough Vineyards Sauvignon Blanc, 2003, Sacred Hill, Marlborough, New Zealand
Silky smooth, rich mouthfeel provides an amazing contrast with the crispness of the wine that tastes of gooseberries and lemons. Delicious, clean, and long.

• Chablis, 2002, Maison Joseph Drouhin, Burgundy, France
Classic aromas of wet stones and earth with flavors of lemon, minerals, nuts, cream, and the faintest hint of cherry vanilla. Tasty and long.

• Les Princes Abbes Riesling, 2001, Domaines Schlumberger, Alsace, France
Extraordinary. Aromas of lime and butterscotch lead to a palate of lime, butter, crushed stones, and orange zest. Beautiful stuff. Dry, crisp, but with excellent concentration, body, and length. Worth every nickel.

• Tokay Pinot Gris, 2001, Domaine du Bollenberg, Alsace, France
Classic Pinot Gris aromas of peach and spice on the nose followed by flavors of full ripe peach with nutmeg, cinnamon, and white pepper. This dry white wine has a full-bodied almost oily mouthfeel with good acidity and excellent balance. Long, concentrated, and drinking well now, but will last until at least 2010.

• St. Romain, 2000, Maison Champy, Burgundy, France
Think freshly baked orange pound cake—all butter, oranges, and toasty caramelized edges.

• Masianco, 2004, Masi, Veneto, Italy
This interesting blend of restrained Pinot Grigio and fruity Verduzzo is both serene and evocative—and bone dry. Pineapple, lemon, and a drizzle of honeyed character on the nose and palate leads to a long, dry, pebble minerality on the finish. Excellent value.

• Chardonnay, 2004, Cono Sur, Santa Elisa Estate and El Marco Estate, Chile
Although Cono Sur positions itself as a modern producer and is indeed relatively new to the wine scene, Cono Sur's single varietal wines display a lot of Old World finesse. The Chardonnay is very Burgundian given its refined flavors, integrated oak, and rich yet elegant mouthfeel. This wine tastes of fresh creamy lemon curd and hints of buttered toast with a long, persistent finish.

• Chardonnay, 2003, Petaluma, Piccadilly Valley, Australia
One big swirl of nectarine, almonds, and creamy vanilla. A favorite of mine.

• Riesling, 2004, Weingut Max Ferd Richte, Mosel, Germany
A wine of serious quality at a titillating price. Crisp Granny Smith apples, lime rind, and warm stones. It's deliciously long with a tight, firm mouthfeel.

• Riesling, 2004, Chateau Ste. Michelle and Dr. Loosen, Washington, USA
Tangerine and wet stones, creamy lemon-lime sherbet. Yum.

• Blanco Reserva, 2000, Marqués de Murrieta, Rioja, Spain
A full-bodied dry wine that's deep in color and tastes of ripe apricots, butterscotch, vanilla, and nuts.

• Zind, 2001, Domaine Zind-Humbrecht, Alsace, France
White pepper and peach nose, followed by a rich spiced peach palate with refreshing acidity, full body, dense fruit, and bone dry finish. Good length. Great today but will keep until about 2009.

• Riesling, 2002, Wegeler Estate, Mosel, Germany
This off-dry wine shows peach and candied lime peel, apricot, and hints of passion fruit. It is beautifully balanced with a seam of good lime-squirt acidity to balance the touch of sweetness. It will develop nicely in bottle until about 2010.

- Riesling "Le Kottabe," 2002, Josmeyer, Alsace, France

This wine is built to last and offers a bowlful of wet pebbles, strips of lemon-lime zest, and a bright streak of acidity. Excellent fruit expression, lean, and long. Will continue to develop until about 2010.

- Rully 1er Cru, 2003, Joseph Drouhin, Burgundy, France

This wine yields a classic flurry of lemon, cream, vanilla, nuts, and toffee flavors at a snip of the price of similar wines from the revered area of France.

- Pinnacles Chardonnay, 2003, Estancia Estate, California, USA

An exhilarating example from Monterey that rings of white Burgundy. It is all finesse and class with fine texture, great balance, gentle almond, and a subtle butteriness threaded with vanilla.

- Seven Hills Sémillon, 2003, L'Ecole No 41, Washington, USA

Lemons and peaches, apricots and cream, caramel and warm stones, and a rich, almost waxy mouthfeel. Gorgeous wine of considerable substance.

- Oom Pagel Sémillon, 2004, Fairview Estate, Paarl, South Africa

Citrus, cream, and almonds with a round, full mouthfeel and lovely lingering finish.

• Sauvage Sauvignon Blanc, 2002, Sacred Hill, Marlborough, New Zealand

This wine has undergone aging in oak, giving it a toasty, nutty flavor beneath the orange, pineapple, and lemon-lime notes. There's also cream and butterscotch flavors that remind me of crème caramel on the finish. Fabulous wine. Drink the latest vintage.

• Dancing Bull Sauvignon Blanc, 2004, Rancho Zabaco, California, USA

All the minerality and freshness of Sauvignon Blanc from great parts of the Loire like Pouilly Fumé, yet this wine is from California. Restrained asparagus, apple, and herb flavors swirl around a firm and intense stony core.

SPARKLING

• Anderson Valley Brut, NV, Roederer Estate, California, USA

From the makers of Cristal in Champagne, this wine is one of the best New World sparkling wines on the market today. It is the closest thing you'll find to Champagne outside of that renowned French region and tastes rich with the hallmarks of Louis Roederer`s exquisite Champagnes—biscuity flavors, toasted brioche, cooked apple, and hints of vanilla, nuts, and butter. Fresh, almost voluptuous, and very refined.

Appendix B: Resources

• Australian Wine & Brandy Corporation
http://www.awbc.com.au

• Australian Government: The Department of Foreign
Affairs and Trade
http://www.dfat.gov.au

• Brigitte Batonnel
Comité Interprofessionnel du Vin de Champagne
France
5, rue Henri Martin
51200 Epernay
France

• Hal Bibby
Amberley & Inniskillin Brand Manager
Vincor Australia Pty Ltd (incorporating Goundrey
& Amberley)
680 Murray Street
PO Box 909, West Perth, WA 6872
Australia

• Blossom Winery
5491 Minoru Boulevard
Richmond, BC V6X 2B1
Canada

• Michael Broadbent
Winetasting, Mitchell Beazley, Great Britain, 2002

• Canadian Vintners Association
www.canadianvintners.com

• Natasha Claxton
R&R Teamwork
'The Basement'
754 Fulham Road,
London SW6 5SH
United Kingdom

• Counseil Interprofessionnel du Vin de Bordeaux
The Guide to Bordeaux Wine, Third Edition, 2003

• Michael Cox
UK Director—Wines of Chile UK Ltd.
13 Hermitage Parade, High Street
Ascot, SL5 7HE
United Kingdom

- *Decanter* magazine
Broadway House
2-6 Fulham Broadway
London SW6 1AA
United Kingdom
www.decanter.com

- John Derrick
Fine Wine Manager
Bibendum Wine Ltd.
113 Regents Park Rd.
London NW1 8UR
United Kingdom

- Isidoro Fernandez-Valmayor
Trade Commission of Spain
2 Floor Street East, Suite 1506
Toronto, ON M4W 1A8
Canada

- Christopher Fielden in association with The
Wine & Education Trust
Exploring Wine & Spirits
Wine & Spirit Education Trust, London, UK, 1994

- Bill Gunn MW
Managing Director
Pol Roger Limited
Shelton House
4 Coningsby Street
Hereford HR1 2DY
United Kingdom

- Jane Holland
Lewis Carroll Communications Inc.
68 Scollard Street
Toronto, Ontario M5R 1G2
Canada

- Gladys Horiuchi
Communications Manager
Wine Institute, California
425 Market Street Suite 1000
San Francisco, CA 94105
USA

- Andrew Jefford
The New France: A Complete Guide to Contemporary French Wine
Mitchell Beazley, Great Britain, 2002

- Natalie Jeune
Focus PR Limited
7-9 Swallow Street
London W1B 4DX
United Kingdom

- Peter Kelsall
Import and Export Coordinator
Vincor Australia Pty Ltd. (Incorporating Goundrey & Amberley)
680 Murray Street
PO Box 909
West Perth, WA 6872
Australia

• Florence Laurent
Champagne Louis Roederer
Service Relations Extérieures
21, boulevard Lundy
51100 Reims
France

• Gérard Liger-Belair
Associate Professor of Physical Sciences
Laboratoire d'oenologie et chimie appliquée
Moulin de la Housse
Université de Reims, BP 1039
51687 Reims, Cedex 2
France

• Martine Lorson
Champagne Louis Roederer
Service Relations Extérieures
21 Boulevard Lundy
51100 Reims
France

• Allison Lu, Manager
Blossom Winery
5491 Minoru Boulevard,
Richmond, BC V6X 2B1
Canada

• Angela Lyons
Public Relations Director
Foster's Wine Estates Canada, Southcorp
5255 Yonge Street, Suite 1111
Toronto, ON M2N 6P4
Canada

• Ian Mitchell
Ne Plus Ultra Agencies
123 Woodfield Road
Toronto, ON M4L 2W5
Canada

• Giovanni Oliva
Export Manager
Bisol
Via Fol 33, 31049 Valdobbiadene (TV)
Italy

• Sylvia Palamoudian
Focus PR Limited
7-9 Swallow Street
London W1B 4DX
United Kingdom

• Kelly Roberts
Communications Coordinator
Washington Wine Commission
93 Pike Street Ste. 315
Seattle, WA 98101
USA

• Jancis Robinson
Oxford Companion to Wine, Second Edition
Oxford University Press, Oxford, UK, 1999

• Jancis Robinson
Vines Grapes & Wines: The Wine Drinker's Guide to Grape Varieties
Mitchell Beazley, Great Britain, 1986

• Jaimi Ruoho
Public Relations Coordinator
Foster's Wine Estates Canada, Southcorp
5255 Yonge Street, Suite 1111
Toronto, ON M2N 6P4
Canada

• Russell Sandham
Brand Manager
The Kirkwood Group
1155 North Service Road West
Unit 5, Oakville, Ontario L6M 3E3
Canada

• Swiss Wine Communication AG
http://www.swisswine.ch

• John Reynolds
Territory Manager, GTA West
The Kirkwood Group
1155 North Service Road West
Unit 5, Oakville, Ontario L6M 3E3
Canada

• Barbara Scalera
Partner
Eviva Communications
International Wine & Spirit Centre
39-45 Bermondsey Street
London SE1 3XF
United Kingdom

• Paul Sullivan
Marketing Manager
Western Wines
1 Hawksworth Road
Telford, Shropshire
United Kingdom

• Sylvia Palamoudian
Focus PR Limited
7-9 Swallow Street
London W1B 4DX
United Kingdom

• Daryl Prefontaine
National Portfolio Manager
Fine Wine Group
Maxxium Canada
1179 King Street West
Toronto, ON M6K 3C5
Canada

• St. Hubertus & Oak Bay Estates Winery
5225 Lakeshore Rd.
Kelowna, BC V1W 4J1
Canada

• Elizabeth Vaughan
Sales & Marketing Coordinator
Pol Roger Limited
Shelton House
4 Coningsby Street
Hereford HR1 2DY
United Kingdom

• Jeremy Watson
The New & Classical Wines of Spain
Montagud, Editores, Barcelona, Spain, 2002

• Chloe Wenban-Smith
Senior Brand Manager
Maisons Marques et Domaines
4 College Mews
St Ann's Hill
London SW18 2S
United Kingdom

• Corrina Wilson
Partner
Eviva Communications
International Wine & Spirit Centre
39-45 Bermondsey Street
London SE1 3XF
United Kingdom

• WineAmerica
1212 New York Avenue, Suite 425
Washington, DC 20005
USA

• Wines of Canada
www.winesofcanada.com

• Jason Woodman
Woodman Wines & Spirits Inc.
523 The Queensway, Suite 1B
Toronto, ON M8Y 1J7
Canada

• Rebecca Yates-Campbell
Assistant Marketing Manager—Public Relations
E & J Gallo Winery Canada
6685 Millcreek Drive, Units 1&2
Mississauga, ON, L5N 5M5
Canada

Index

A

40, 42, 43, 45; Yellow Label Cabernet Sauvignon 2002, 289; [yellowtail] wines, 237; Zind, 103, 292

Aconcagua region, 229

A Crux, 233

Ada Nada, 130

Adegas Morgadío, 158

aeration, 49, 50. *See also* decanting

age/aging: aromas and, 42; Bordeaux wines, 67, 72; Cabernet Sauvignon, 60; Champagne, 94, 95; Château Gruaud-Larose, 64; Chenin Blanc, 107; drinking times and, 29–34, 45; Eola Hills Pinot Noir wines, 209; Madeira, 175; oak, 42, 43, 89; Tawny Ports, 171; wine and food pairing, 27; wine labels and, 30; wine serving, 47; wine tasting and, 39

Aglianico, 148

Aglianico d'Irpina, 148

air, exposure to, 266

Albariño, 6–7, 158

Albet i Noya, 158

alcohol: aging and, 31; Australian wines, 235; Barolo, 129; California wines, 206; Champagne, 92; Dr. Unger Riesling Reserve 2002, 184; German wines, 178; Gewurztraminer, 101; legs and, 40; maturity and, 29, 30; Moscato d'Asti, 133; Muscadet, 106; Oloroso Sherry, 163; Port, 170; Sherry, 165; Swiss wines, 188; Valpolicella Superiore, 135; Vin Doux Naturel, 125; wine and food pairing, 23; wine flaws and, 53; wine labels and, 35; wine storage and, 265; wine tasting and, 44, 45

Alentejo region, 167, 168, 169, 287

Alexander Valley AVA, 203

and, 41, 42; primary and secondary, 42; wine faults and, 51, 52, 53–54; wine glasses and, 49. *See also specific aromas*

Artadi, 152

Artist Series Cabernet Sauvignon, 212

Artist Series Cabernet Sauvignon 2001, 289

asparagus (flavor/aroma), 9; American wines, 200; Dancing Bull Sauvignon Blanc 2004, 294; French wines, 127; South African wines, 249; wine and food pairing, 26

assemblage, 59

Assyrtiko, 194, 195

Asti, 132, 133

Aszú, 189

Atkins, Tim, 272

attack, 277

Atwater Vineyards, 215

auction houses, 17

Auguste Clape, 116

auslese wines, 179

Australia, 12, 57; Argentina and, 232; wine and food pairing, 25; wines of, 235–41; wines under $20, 285, 287, 288, 289, 292

Australian Government: The Department of Foreign Affairs and Trade, 295

Australian Wine & Brandy Corporation, 295

Austrian wines, 11, 183–85

Auxerrois (red grape). *See* Malbec

Auxerrois (white grape), 7

Auxerrois Gris, 7. *See also* Pinot Gris

B

Bacchus, 7

Baco Noir, 4, 220

Badger Mountain Vineyard, 213

balance, 31; Bin 28 Shiraz 2001, 288; Chilean wines, 226; Inniskillin Vidal Icewine 2003, 221; Pinnacles Chardonnay 2003, 293; St. Hubertus Estate Chasselas 2005, 220; Sherry, 161; Shiraz Show Reserve 1998, 288; Tokay Pinot Gris 2001 (Domaine de Bollenberg), 291; wine tasting and, 45; Yellow Label Cabernet Sauvignon 2002, 289

Balmur area, 77

banana (flavor/aroma), 4, 42, 87

bandage aroma, 53

Bandol area, 121

Banks, Charles, 198

Banyuls, 125

Barbadillo, 165

Barbaresco, 56, 129, 130–31

barbecued pepper steak (flavor/aroma), 212

barbecued steak (flavor/aroma), 289

Barbera, 4, 131–32

Barbera d'Alba, 131

Barbera d'Asti, 131, 132

Barbera del Piedmonte, 131

Barbour Vineyards, 199

Barca Velha, 168

Barolo, 10, 20, 23, 45, 56, 129–30, 143

Barone Ricasoli, 141

Baron Philippe de Rothschild SA, 73, 207, 228, 285

Barossa Valley, 238, 287

barrel toast, 278

Barrett, Heidi, 198–99

Barsac, 26, 70, 72, 73, 119

basil (flavor/aroma), 101

black pepper (flavor/aroma), 5, 6, 11; American
    wines, 207, 211, 212; Australian wines, 239;
    French wines, 73, 112, 121; Italian wines, 148,
    149; Petalos del Bierzo 2004, 286; Reserva
    Alentejo 2001, 287; Spanish wines, 159; Tatone
    Montepulciano d'Abuzzo 2000, 288
black peppercorns (flavor/aroma), 289
black plum (flavor/aroma), 4, 5, 123, 135, 285
black raspberry (flavor/aroma), 207
black stone fruit (flavor/aroma), 118, 123, 129,
    233
Black Tower, 181
black truffle (flavor/aroma), 62, 82, 233
blackberry (flavor/aroma), 4, 5, 6; American
    wines, 203, 209, 210; Castillo Ygay Tinto Gran
    Reserva 2001, 289; French wines, 73, 112, 123;
    Italian wines, 133, 146, 149; Merlot 2004 (Cono
    Sur), 286; South African wines, 248; Tatone
    Montepulciano d'Abuzzo 2000, 288; Zinfandel
    Vintners Blend 2003, 288
blackberry liqueur (flavor/aroma), 237
blanc de blancs Champagne, 91
blanc de noirs Champagne, 91
Blanchot area, 77
Blanco Reserva, 153
Blanco Reserva 2000, 292
Blanco Seco, 153
Blanquette de Limoux, 124
Blauburgunder, 187
Blaye, 68
blended wines, 261
blood (flavor/aroma), 211
Blossom Winery, 222, 296, 299
blueberries (flavor/aroma), 4, 6; American

butterscotch (flavor/aroma), 57, 153, 222, 240, 244, 290, 292, 294

Buzet, 122

C

Cabernet d'Anjou, 110

Cabernet Franc, 4; aging, 30; Bordeaux region, 59, 68, 70; Canadian Icewines, 222; Chile, 226; Loire region, 106, 108, 110, 111; New York state, 214; Southwest France, 122

Cabernet Merlot, Australia, 237, 240

Cabernet Sauvignon, 3, 4, 10, 17, 23; aging, 30; Argentina, 233; Australia, 237; Bordeaux region, 59, 60; Bordeaux region, 67, 68, 70; Chile, 226, 227, 228, 229; France, 57; Greece, 194; Italy, 134, 139, 142, 143; Languedoc region, 124; Loire region, 106, 110; South Africa, 248; Southwest France, 122; Spanish wines, 156, 157; United States, 199, 201, 207, 212, 214

Cabernet Sauvignon 2002 (Wynn's Coonawarra Estate), 285

Cabernet Sauvignon 2005 (Casillero del Diablo), 285

Cadillac, 73

Cahors, 123

Caiarossa, 144

California: France and, 57, 58; wine tasting, 44; wines of, 197–208; wines under $20, 288, 293, 294

Calvet, 74

Calvet Reserve Rouge 2002, 287

Campania, 147, 148

Campofiorin, 137

Campofiorin 2002, 285

Chevalier-Montrachet, 80

Chianti, 10, 36, 140, 141, 142

Chianti Classico, 140, 141, 142

Chianti Classico Riservas, 141

Chianti Rufina, 142

Chianti Rufina Reserva, 284

Chilean wines, 11, 57, 58, 225–30, 285, 286, 291

chilling, 47, 98

China, 253

Chinon, 111

chocolate (flavor/aroma), 57; American wines, 199, 207, 210, 211; Australian wines, 236, 239; Cabernet Sauvignon 2002 (Wynn's Coonawarra Estate), 285; Carménère 2004 (Casillero del Diablo), 286; Chilean wines, 228; Escudo Rojo 2002, 285; French wines, 63, 64, 84, 113; Italian wines, 130, 136, 140, 143, 149; Merlot 2004 (Cono Sur), 286; Portuguese wines, 168; Spanish wines, 152, 154

Churchill Cellars Ltd., 275

Cicchetti, 138

cigar box (flavor/aroma), 207, 233

cigars (flavor/aroma), 56

cinnamon (flavor/aroma), 11, 102, 145, 152, 154, 211, 213, 291

Cinsault, 4, 112, 117, 119, 120

citrus (flavor/aroma), 3, 7, 9; American wines, 211; Australian wines, 238; Bisol Prosecco di Valdobbiandene Crede, 137; Canadian wines, 221, 222; Italian wines, 134, 137; Oom Pagel Sémillon 2004, 293; South African wines, 248

citrus fruit (flavor/aroma), 237

citrus zest (flavor/aroma), 101, 116, 195, 221

Clairette, 7, 112, 120

Crusted Port, 33, 172
Cullen Wines, 241
cuvée, 96
Cuvée Julien Brut, 103
Cuvée No 729, 95
Cuvée Sir Winston Churchill, 96
Cyprus, 194

D

Dalla Valle Vineyards, 197, 199
Dalmau Tinto Reserva, 152
Dancing Bull Sauvignon Blanc 2004, 200, 294
dark berries (flavor/aroma), 226, 285
dark chocolate (flavor/aroma), 5, 6, 56; American wines, 207; Argentinian wines, 233; Australian wines, 239; French wines, 112, 117; Italian wines, 148; Koonunga Hill Shiraz Cabernet, 287; Merlot 2002 (Pikes), 289; Rasteau 2003, 284; Shiraz Show Reserve 1998, 288; Spanish wines, 154; Tatone Montepulciano d'Abuzzo 2000, 288
dark fruit (flavor/aroma), 245, 287
David Léclapart, 99
Decanter.com, 201
Decanter magazine, 269, 271, 273, 274, 297
decanting, 49–50, 171, 173, 174, 257, 260
demi-sec, 93
Derrick, John, 297
Descendientes de Jose Palacios, 159, 160, 286
Désirée Chocolate Dessert Wine, 204
dessert wines, 13, 128, 240. See also specific wines
Deutz, 95
Deuziemes Crus, 71
DFJ Vinhos, 169

Dundee Hills, 209
duties, 14

E

F

157, 163, 166, 184, 205, 249, 258, 259, 288. *See also* restaurants

foot treading, 170

forest fruits (flavor/aroma), 4; Australian wines, 239; Canadian wines, 220; French wines, 63, 64, 83; Italian wines, 135, 143; Petalos del Bierzo 2004, 286; Spanish wines, 159

fortified wines, 33. *See also* Madeira

Foster's Wine Estates Canada, 299, 301

fourth growth wines, 62

France. *See* French wines

Franciscan Estates, 199

François Lumpp, 85

Freiherr Heyl zu Herrnsheim, 181

Freixenet, 156

French oak, 11, 151

Frenchtown, Washington, 212

French wines, 28, 56, 127–28, 188; Alsacean wines, 100–105; Bordeaux wines, 59–75; Burgundy wines, 75–90; Champagne wines, 90–100; guide to, 273; Languedoc and Roussillon wines, 124–26; Loire wines, 106–11; Provence and Corsica wines, 120–22; Rhône wines, 111–19; Southwestern wines, 122–23; Vin de Pays, 126–27; wines under $20, 283, 284, 287, 290, 291, 292, 293

Frescobaldi, 142

freshness, 30, 59

Frey Vineyards, 208

Friuli-Venezia region, 138, 139

Frogs Leap Winery, 208

Fronsac, 68

fruit (flavor/aroma), 44

fruitcake (flavor/aroma), 287

fruit concentration, 29, 30, 42, 44, 45; aging and, 31; Australian wines, 235; Barolo, 129; California wines, 206; Campofiorin 2002, 285; Château Grand Mayne, 64; Château Grand-Puy Ducasse, 63–64; Château Gruaud-Larose, 64; Château Lynch-Bages, 62; Château Pontet-Canet, 62; Chilean wines, 226; Hiru Tres Racimos, 152; Inniskillin Vidal Icewine 2003, 221; Jackson Triggs Vidal Icewine 2003, 221; Kuwala Chardonnay 2004, 250; Les Princes Abbes Riesling, 101; Les Princes Abbes Riesling 2001, 290; Oloroso Sherry, 163; Paso Robles Cabernet Sauvignon wines, 207; Riesling "Le Kottabe" 2002, 103, 293; St. Hubertus Estate Chasselas 2005, 220; Tatone Montepulciano d'Abuzzo 2000, 288; "Uncut Shiraz," 238; wine storage and, 265; [yellowtail] wines, 237; Y series wines, 238; Zind, 103; Zind 2001, 292
fruit wines, 222
fruity wines, 12
full-bodied wines, alcohol level of, 35
Fumé Blanc. *See* Sauvignon Blanc
fungicides, 89, 154, 219
Furmint, 7, 190

G

Gamay, 4, 34; aging, 30; Burgundy region, 76, 86, 89; Loire region, 106, 108, 110; Switzerland, 187; wine myths, 258
Gamay Beaujolais, 4, 202
Gambero Rosso (Italian wine guide), 149, 273
game (flavor/aroma), 5, 42, 82, 83, 84
Gamla, 194
garagiste, 248, 279

Garganega, 136
Garnacha, 5, 151, 157
gasoline (flavor/aroma), 9, 180
Gavi, 133–34
Gemtree, 238, 241
generic wines, 15
Georges Deboeuf, 88, 283
geraniums (aroma), 53
Germany, 8, 11, 57–58; Swiss wines and, 188; wines of, 177–81; wines under $20, 292
Gewurztraminer (Alsacean), 100, 101–102, 104
Gewürztraminer, 7, 25, 214, 259
Giacomo Bologna, 132
gifts, wine as, 267–69
Gigondas, 117, 118
Gildas Cormerais Muscadet de Sèvre et Maine 2004, Sur Lie, 107
Ginestet (Bordeaux négociant), 68
Givery area, 85
glasses. See wine glasses
global warming, 254
glue (aroma), 54
Goats do Roam Red, 247
Golan, 194
Golan Heights Winery, 194
Golden Delicious apple (flavor/aroma), 7
González Byass, 162, 165
gooseberries (flavor/aroma), 9, 127, 244, 249, 290
Grace, Dick, 199
Grace Family Cabernet Sauvignon 2003, 199
Grace Family Vineyards, 197, 199, 208
Graham Beck Brut Rosé, 250
Grand Cru (Alsacean classification), 105
Grand Cru (Bordeaux classification), 66, 67

Israel, 193–94

Italian wines, 8, 56–57; Central Italy, 145–47; guide to, 273; Northeast Italy, 134–39; Northwest Italy, 129–34; Southern Italy and the islands, 147–49; Tuscany, 139–45; wine and food pairing, 24; wine merchants and, 274; wines under $20, 284, 285, 288, 291

J

Jackson-Triggs, 221, 222

Jacquesson, 95, 99

Japan, 253

Jardin Winery, 249

Jasper Hill Winery, 241

Jean-Marc Brocard

Jefford, Andrew, 273, 298

Jerez region, 161, 162

Jermann, Silvio, 138

Jermann Pinot Grigio, 138

Jeune, Natalie, 298

João Portugal Ramos, 169

Johnson, Hugh, 274

Jordan Vineyards, 250

Jordan Winery, 249

Joseph Drouhin, 76, 84, 290, 293

Josmeyer, 103, 293

Judean Hills, 193

Jugla family, 65

Jumilla, 161

Jura area, 127–28

K

Kelsall, Peter, 298

Kerner, 7, 180

South African wines, 249; Spanish wines, 159
lemon curd (flavor/aroma), 9, 291
lemon fruit (flavor/aroma), 159
lemon-lime (flavor/aroma), 244, 294
lemon-lime sherbet (flavor/aroma), 292
lemon-lime zest (flavor/aroma), 293
lemon oil (flavor/aroma), 158
lemon squirt (flavor/aroma), 291
lemon-squirt sour (flavor/aroma), 10
lemon zest (flavor/aroma), 82, 146, 221
Le Montrachet, 81
Le Musigny, 80
length, 16, 45; Campofiorin 2002, 285; Castillo
   Ygay Tinto Gran Reserva 2001, 289; Chablis
   2002 (Maison Joseph Drouhin), 290; Château
   Beau-Sejour Becot, 63; Château Canon-la-
   Gaffeliere, 63; Château Giscours, 63; Château
   Grand Mayne, 64; Château Grand-Puy
   Ducasse, 64; Château Gruaud-Larose, 64;
   Château Kirwan, 64; Château Lynch-Bages, 62;
   Château Pontet-Canet, 62; Château Talbot, 63;
   Domaine du Viking Vouvray 2001, 108;
   Inniskillin Vidal Icewine 2003, 221; Jackson
   Triggs Vidal Icewine 2003, 221; L'Ecole No 41
   Cabernet Sauvignon 2001, 212; Les Princes
   Abbes Riesling, 101; Les Princes Abbes Ries-
   ling 2001, 290; Marlborough Vineyards Sauvi-
   gnon Blanc 2003, 290; Marquês de Borba 2003,
   169; Masianco 2004, 291; Morgenhof Chenin
   Blanc 2004, 249; Oom Pagel Sémillon 2004,
   293; Riesling "Le Kottabe" 2002, 103, 293; Ries-
   ling Saering 2004, 101; Riesling 2004 (Weingut
   Max Ferd Richte), 292; Rubesco Reserva, 146;
   St. Hubertus Estate Chasselas 2005, 220; Tokay

Pinot Gris 2001 (Domaine de Bollenberg), 291; Yellow Label Cabernet Sauvignon 2002, 289; [yellowtail] Cabernet Sauvignon 2005, 237; Zind, 103, 292

Léon, Patrick, 66

Léon Béyer, 102

Leonetti Cellar, 212

Le petit Domaine de Gimios, 126

L'Ermita, 157

Les Beauroy, 77

Les Carruades de Lafite, 65

Les Clos, 77, 79

Les Cortons, St. Auben 1er Cru 2002, 83

Les Forts de Latour, 65

Les Fourchaumes area, 77

Les Montmains area, 77

Les Princes Abbes Riesling, 101

Les Princes Abbes Riesling 2001, 290

Les Terrasses, 157, 160

Les Vaillons area, 77

Les Vaudevey area, 77

Levin Sauvignon Blanc 2004 Vin de Pays du Jardin de la France, 127

Lewis Carroll Communications Inc., 298

licorice (flavor/aroma), 62, 113, 129, 239, 284, 287

liebraumilch, 181

Lifford Wine Agency, 275

Liger-Belair, Gérard, 258, 299

light-bodied wines, alcohol level of, 35

light exposure, 265

Lilbert, 99

Limarí region, 229

lime (flavor/aroma), 7, 8, 9; American wines, 211; Austrian wines, 183, 184; Canadian

Mâconnais region, 76, 85, 86

Mâcon-Supérieur, 85, 86

Mâcon-Villages, 86

Madeira, 33, 36, 57, 174–75

magnum, wines in, 32

Magrez, Bernard, 65

Maipo region, 228, 229, 285, 286

Maison Champy, 83, 291

Maison Chapoutier, 119

Maison Joseph Drouhin. See Joseph Drouhin

Maisons Marques et Domaines, 303

Malaga, wine labels and, 36

Malbec, 5, 10; Argentina, 231, 233; Bordeaux region, 59, 70; Loire region, 106; Southwest France, 122, 123; Spain, 156

Malibu-Netwon Canyon AVA, 203

Malmsey, 175

Malmsey Madeira, 174, 175

malolactic fermentation, 53, 280

Malvasia, 7, 144, 145

Manara, 137

mango chutney (flavor/aroma), 221

Manzanilla, 32, 162, 166

maple syrup (flavor/aroma), 215

Marche region, 145

Marchesi Antinori, 142

Margaret River, 240

markups. See restaurant markups

Marlborough, 243, 244, 290, 294

Marlborough Vineyards Sauvignon Blanc 2003, 290

marmalade (flavor/aroma), 72, 189, 245

Marnier Lapostolle, 227

Marquês de Borba 2003, 169

mixed berries (flavor/aroma), 4, 5, 6, 86, 111, 120, 133, 151

mixed citrus (flavor/aroma), 7, 211

mixed forest fruits (flavor/aroma), 83, 135, 239

mixed spices (flavor/aroma), 5

mocha (flavor/aroma), 84, 228, 285

Moët & Chandon, 96, 98

Molinara, 134

Monastrell, 5

Mondavi, 207, 226

Montagny area, 85

Montbazillac area, 122

Montepulciano, 5, 145, 146

Montepulciano d'Abruzzo, 146

Monterey AVA, 202, 203

Montirius, 119

Morgenhof, 249

Moscatel, 161. *See also* Muscat

Moscato, 133. *See also* Muscat

Moscato d'Asti, 133

Mosel, 180, 292

Moselle, 36

Moulin-à-Vent Fleur 2004, 283

Mount Riley, 244

Mount Veeder, 207

Mountain Vintners Estate Cabernet Sauvignon 1999, 213

Mourvèdre, 5, 53, 112, 117, 120, 121, 124

Mousse, 92

mouthfeel, 37; Bin 28 Kalimna Shiraz, 239; Chardonnay 2004 (Cono Sur), 291; Château Talbot, 63; Escudo Rojo, 228; Escudo Rojo 2002, 285; Marlborough Vineyards Sauvignon Blanc 2003, 290; Meritage 2003, 219; Merlot 2002

(Pikes), 289; Oom Pagel, 248; Oom Pagel Sémillon 2004, 293; Riesling 2004 (Weingut Max Ferd Richte), 292; Riesling Steinmassel 2002, 184; Seven Hills Semillon 2003, 293; Tokay Pinot Gris 2001 (Domaine de Bollenberg), 291; wine tasting and, 42; Y series wines, 238
Mouton Cadet, 73
Mouton Cadet Blanc, 73
Mouton Cadet Graves Sec, 73
Mouton Cadet Médoc Reserve, 73
Mouton Cadet Rosé, 74
Mouton Cadet Rouge, 73
Mouvedre, 211
Movia, 191
Mud House Wines, 245
Müller-Thurgau, 8, 180, 187, 253, 260
Muscadel, 247
Muscadelle, 8, 59, 70
Muscadet, 8, 24, 27, 106–7, 260
Muscadet Sur Lie, 107
Muscat, 8, 100, 102, 103, 119, 125, 201
Muscat Canelli, 199
Muscat d'Alsace, 103
mushroom (flavor/aroma), 6, 42, 82, 83, 84, 108
musk (flavor/aroma), 7
must, 280
musty aromas, 41, 52

N

Nahe region, 180
nail polish remover (aroma), 54
Napa Gamay, 5, 202
Napa Valley, 199, 207
Napa Valley Wine Auction, 198

Napoleon Seco, 162
Nativa, 229
Navara region, 157
Nebbiolo, 5, 10, 30, 129
nectarine (flavor/aroma), 238, 292
négociants, 75, 76, 281
Neil Ellis Chardonnay 2003, 250
Neil Ellis Sauvignon Blanc 2005, 249
Nepenthe Wines, 240
Ne Plus Ultra Agencies, 275, 300
neutral aroma (flavor/aroma), 7, 8, 9
Nevers forest, 89
New & Classical Wines of Spain, The (Watson), 303
New France, The (Jefford), 273, 298
New World wines, 12, 21, 35, 261. *See also specific countries, regions, and wines*
New York wines, 214–15
New Zealand, 58, 79, 243–45, 290, 294
Niagara region, 217
Nicholas Potel, 84
Niebaum-Coppola Estate Winery, 200, 201
Nikolaihof Wachau, 185
Nipozzano, Frescobaldi 2002, 284
Nipozzano Riserva, 142
noble rot, 70, 185, 281
Nord-Sud Viognier, 127
North America, 12
Northeast Italy, wines of, 134–39
Northeast Spain, wines of, 156–58
Northwest Italy, wines of, 129–34
Northwest Spain, wines of, 158–60
Norton, 233
nose. *See* aromas
nosing wines, 41–42

Nuits St. Georges, 83

Nuragus, 8, 148

nutmeg (flavor/aroma), 102, 291

nuts (flavor/aroma), 7, 9, 27, 33, 57; American wines, 205, 212; Anderson Valley Brut, NV, 294; Austrian wines, 184; Blanco Reserva 2000, 292; Canadian wines, 221; Chablis 2002 (Maison Joseph Drouhin), 290; Chilean wines, 229; French wines, 63, 64, 84, 94, 95, 104, 109; Italian wines, 138, 146; Portuguese wines, 174; Rully 1er Cru 2003, 293; Sauvage Sauvignon Blanc 2002, 294; Spanish wines, 153, 159, 162, 163

O

oak (flavor/aroma), 250

oak barrels, 11

oak chips, 11

oak essence, 11

oak staves, 11

Observatory, The, 248

O. Founrier, 233

Okanogan Valley, 217, 219

old wines, 49, 50, 262

Old World wines, 12, 24, 35, 261. *See also specific countries, regions, and wines*

olfactory glands, 41

Oliva, Giovanni, 300

olive (flavor/aroma), 239, 287

Olivier Cousin, 111

Oloroso Jerez Extra Viejo 1/7, 165

Oloroso Sherry, 161, 163, 166

Ontario, 217, 218, 219, 275

Ontario Imported Wine-Spirit-Beer Association,

Palacio de Menade, 159
Palacios, Alvaro, 153, 154, 157, 160
Palamoudian, Sylvia, 300, 302
Palomino, 161
Paradigm Winery, 199
Parellada, 8, 156
Paris, 28, 128
Parker, Robert, Jr., 198, 273
Paso Robles, 207
passion fruit (flavor/aroma), 180, 292
pastry (flavor/aroma), 95
Patianna Organic Vineyards, 208
Pauillac, 56, 65
Pavillon Rouge du Château Margaux, 65
peach (flavor/aroma), 7, 8, 9; Argentinian wines,
    232; Austrian wines, 184; Canadian wines,
    220; French wines, 62, 72, 102, 103, 107, 113,
    116, 120, 127; Italian wines, 138; Riesling 2002
    (Wegeler Estate), 292; Seven Hills Semillon
    2003, 293; Spanish wines, 158; Tokay Pinot
    Gris 2001 (Domaine de Bollenberg), 291; Zind
    2001, 292
pear (flavor/aroma), 9, 127, 137, 221
pebbles (flavor/aroma), 113
pecans (flavor/aroma), 83
Pedro Domecq, 163
Pedro Ximénez, 161
Pedro Ximénez Sherry, 163
Pellegrini Winery and Vineyards, 215
pencil shavings (flavor/aroma), 4, 74, 287
Penfolds, 238, 239, 240, 288
Penfolds Grange, 238, 239
Penfolds Koonunga Hill, 239
pepper (flavor/aroma), 84, 101, 102, 113, 213,

Pinot Bianco, 136

Pinot Blanc, 8, 23; Alsace, 100, 102; Austria, 183; pairing foods with, 27; United States, 201, 214

Pinot Grigio, 8, 138, 260

Pinot Gris, 8, 31, 100, 102, 138, 180

Pinot Meunier, 90, 91, 156, 262

Pinot Noir, 4, 5–6, 16, 25, 26; aging, 30; Alsace region, 100, 102; Australia, 240; Bouzy Rouge, 127; Burgundy region, 76, 79, 82, 83, 84, 85, 88, 89; Champagne wines, 90, 91, 95; Chile, 227; Germany, 180; Loire region, 106, 109; New Zealand, 244, 245; South Africa, 250; Spain, 156; Switzerland, 187; United States, 202, 208–10, 213; wine myths, 262

Pinotage, 5, 25, 248

pips, 43

place, 18

plastic corks, 264

Platinum Label Barossa Shiraz 2002, 236

plum (flavor/aroma), 4; American wines, 209, 211; Cabernet Sauvignon 2005 (Casillero del Diablo), 285; Carménère 2004 (Casillero del Diablo), 286; Chilean wines, 227, 228; Escudo Rojo 2002, 285; French wines, 82, 123; Italian wines, 130, 135, 146, 149; Merlot 2004 (Cono Sur), 286; New Zealand wines, 244, 245; Portuguese wines, 169; Reserva Alentejo 2001, 287; Spanish wines, 154

Pocket Wine Guide (Johnson), 274

Poggio Trevvalle, 144

Pol Roger, 96, 98, 99

Pol Roger Brut Reserve, 95

Pol Roger Champagne, 93

Pol Roger Limited, 297, 302

red plum (flavor/aroma), 4, 134, 212, 285, 289

Red Reserva, 152

Red Reserva 2000, 287

red roses (flavor/aroma), 6

red stone fruit (flavor/aroma), 129

red wines, 10, 19, 20; aging and, 30; maturity, 40; myths about, 258, 260, 262; pairing foods with, 25, 26; serving, 47, 48, 50; tannins, 43; under $20, 283–89; wine faults, 53. *See also specific wines*

Regaleali estate, 147

regional grape varieties, 14. *See also specific regions and varieties*

regional wines, 24, 36. *See also specific regions and wines*

Reims, 90

Remelluri, 154

Reserva Alentejo, 168

Reserva Alentejo 2001, 287

Reserve de La Comtesse, 64

Reserve Merlot 2001 (Vina Carmen), 286

restaurant markups, 21, 22

restaurants, 15, 19–22, 28

retail margins, 14

Retsina, 195

Revana Family Vineyard, 199

Reyneke Wines, 251

Reynolds, John, 301

Rhine, 36

Rhône region, 25, 53, 111–19, 227

rhubarb (flavor/aroma), 101, 239

Rias Baixas, 158, 160

Ribatejo region, 167, 169

Ribbon Ridge, 209, 210

Roederer Estate, 205, 294
Rolland, Michel, 65, 191
Rolle, 9, 120
Romanée-Conti, 80
Romanée-St-Vivant, 80
Rondinella, 134, 137
rose (flavor/aroma), 5, 6, 7, 42; American wines,
   210; French wines, 64, 101; Italian wines, 129,
   130; Portuguese wines, 169
Rosé d'Anjou, 110
Rosé de Loire, 110
rose petals (flavor/aroma), 104, 205
rosé wines, 10, 25, 28, 33, 34, 47. *See also specific
   wines*
Rosenblum Cellars, 204, 205
rotten eggs (aroma), 53
Roussanne, 9, 111, 112, 114, 115
Roussillon, wines of, 124–26
Rozendal Farm, 251
Rubesco Reserva, 146
Rubicon, 200
Ruby Port, 172
Ruchottes-Chambertin, 80
Rueda Blanco, 159
Rueda region, 159
Rufina, 142
Ruinart, 98, 99
Ruländer, 9, 180
Rully, 84, 85
Rully 1er Cru 2003, 84, 293
Ruoho, Jaimi, 301

S

pairing foods with, 26, 72; Rhône region, 119; wine labels and, 36

Sauvage, 244

Sauvage Sauvignon Blanc 2002, 294

Sauvignon (perfume), 68

Sauvignon Blanc, 9, 10; Argentina, 232; aromas, 41; Bordeaux region, 59, 70, 73; Burgundy region, 88; Chile, 228; Greece, 194; Languedoc region, 124; Loire region, 106, 108, 109; New Zealand, 243, 244; Northeast Italy, 134; pairing foods with, 25, 26; South Africa, 249; Spain, 159; United States, 200, 201, 214

Sauvignon Blanc 2003 (Robertson Winery), 290

Savennieres Roche aux Moines 1999, 107

Savoie, 128

Scalera, Barbara, 301

Schäfer-Fröhlich, 180

Scheurebe, 9, 180

Schloss Wallhaüsen, 181

Screaming Eagle Winery, 197, 198, 199

screwcaps, 264

seasons, 11

secondary aromas, 42

second growths, 61, 71

second wines, 64–65, 281

sediment, 49, 172

Seghesio Old Vine Zinfandel, 205

Seifried, 245

Sélection de Grain Nobles, 104

Selosse, 99

Sémillon, 9, 59, 70, 120, 212, 248, 249

Seña, 226, 230

Senderens, Alain, 28

Sercial, 175

Alentejo 2001, 287; Sauvignon Blanc 2003 (Robertson Winery), 290; South African wines, 248; Spanish wines, 152, 154, 159

smoked meat (flavor/aroma), 123, 239

smoked pear (flavor/aroma), 249

smoky cherries (flavor/aroma), 148

smoky meats (flavor/aroma), 287

smoky wines, 25

Soave, 134, 136

Soave DOC, 136

Sofia Mini Blanc de Blancs, 201

Sogrape, 168, 169, 287

soil: France, 76, 79, 89, 109; Israel, 193; Italy, 142; Santorini, 195; Spain, 154

soil erosion, 89

sommelier, 20

Sommeliers Series, 48

Sonoma County, 205

sour (flavor/aroma), 9

sour cherries (flavor/aroma), 63, 289

sour lemon (flavor/aroma), 9

sour wines, 11, 25, 27. *See also specific wines*

sourness. *See* acidity

South African wines, 25, 247–51, 290, 293

South America, 12. *See also specific countries, regions, and wines*

Southern Italy, wines of, 147–49

Southwest France, wines of, 122–23

Spanish wines, 28, 57; Central and Southern Spain, 160–61; Northeast Spain, 156–58; Northwest Spain, 158–60; Ribera del Duero, 155–56; Rioja, 151–55; Sherry, 161–66; under $20, 283, 286, 287, 289, 292; wine merchants and, 274

storage. *See* wine storage

straw (flavor/aroma), 7

strawberry (flavor/aroma), 4, 5, 6, 42, 57, 74, 152, 157

structure, 37, 43; Château Canon-la-Gaffeliere, 63; Château Gruaud-Larose, 64; Château Kirwan, 64; Château Lynch-Bages, 62; Château Pontet-Canet, 62; Château Talbot, 63; Propiedad 2003, 154; St. Hippolyte 2002, 101; Seven Hills Merlot 2001, 212

sugar, 42, 43, 57, 92

Sullivan, Paul, 302

sulphur, 54

summer berries (flavor/aroma), 157

Summerhill Pyramid Winery, 223

supermarkets, 15

Supertuscan wines, 139–40

süss wines, 184

sweat (flavor/aroma), 62

Swedish Hill, 215

sweet Champagne, 93

sweet cherry (flavor/aroma), 146, 205, 219

sweetness, 40, 42

sweet Vouvray, 108

sweet wines, 26, 27, 47, 57. *See also specific wines*

Swiss Wine Communication AG, 301

Swiss wines, 187–88

Sylvaner/Silvaner, 9, 27, 100, 180, 187, 260

Syrah/Shiraz, 6; Australia, 238, 239; Chile, 227, 229; Greece, 194; Italy, 142; Languedoc region, 124; pairing food with, 23, 25; Portugal, 169; Rhône region, 112, 114, 115, 116, 117; South Africa, 248; Spain, 157; United States, 199, 211

Szepsy, 190

T

Trebbiano, 9, 41, 56, 136, 144, 145, 146
Trebbiano d'Abruzzo, 146
Trebbiano di Soave, 136
Trebbiano Toscano, 136
Trentino, 131, 144
Trimbach, 104
Trinity Hill, 245
trockenbeerenauslese wines, 178, 184
trocken wines, 184
Trollinger, 6, 180
tropical fruit (flavor/aroma), 159, 184, 221
Trotte Vieille, 67
truffle (flavor/aroma), 6, 83, 84, 149, 209
Turkey Flat, 241
Turriga IGT, 149
Tuscany, wines of, 139–45
typicity, 13
Tyrrell's, 241

U

Ugni Blanc, 112, 120. *See also* Trebbiano
Ull de Llebre. *See* Tempranillo
Umbria, 146
"Uncut Shiraz," 238
Único, 155
United States: California wines, 197–208; Canadian wine and, 218; New York wines, 214–215; Oregon, Washington, and Idaho wines, 208–13; Pinot Noir, 79; Virginia wines, 216; wine labels and, 36; wines under $20, 287, 288, 289, 292, 293, 294
unoaked Chardonnay, 10, 25. *See also* Chardonnay
Upper Galilee, 193
Uruguay, 254

V

waiters, 20, 22

Wales, 253

Walla Walla Valley AVA, 211, 212, 287

Walla Walla Vintners, 212

walnuts (flavor/aroma), 63

warm stones (flavor/aroma), 284, 292, 293

Washington Wine Commission, 300

Washington wines, 208–13, 287, 289, 292, 293

Watson, Jeremy, 303

weather, 11

websites, 13

weddings, wines served at, 87

Wegeler Estate, 292

Wegeler Estate Riesling 2002, 180

Weingut Brundlemayer, 183, 184

Weingut Geyerhof, 185

Weingut Max Ferd Richter, 180, 292

Weingut Schönberger, 185

Wenban-Smith, 303

Western Wines, 302

wet pebbles (flavor/aroma), 73, 103, 293

wet stones (flavor/aroma), 249, 290, 292

white Burgundy, 202

white flowers (flavor/aroma), 7, 8, 9; Canadian wines, 220; French wines, 64, 73, 101, 107, 116, 120; Reserve Merlot 2001 (Vina Carmen), 286

white grape varieties, 3, 6–9, 10. *See also specific varieties*

White Grenache (flavor/aroma), 5

white peach (flavor/aroma), 8, 116

white pepper (flavor/aroma), 11, 103, 205, 209, 219, 291, 292

white Port, 171

white Sancerre, 109

ling, 245

winemaking process and techniques, 10, 17, 42

wine merchants, 12, 14, 15, 17; Barbera, 132; Burgundy wines, 75; drinking times, 31, 32; secrets about, 274–75

wine myths, 257–62

wine producers, 13, 14, 15, 17, 55. *See also* biodynamic viticulture; organic wine producers; *specific producers*

wine purchasing, 3–18

wine resources, 271–75, 295–304

wine retailers, 15, 17

wines: chilling, 47, 98; drinking times for, 29–34, 39; faulty, 51–54; filtering, 40; as gifts, 267–69; nosing, 41–42; ordering, 19–22; pairing food with, 23–28; ready-to drink, 20; serving, 37, 47–50; under $20, 283–94

Wine Society, The, 269, 272

Wines of Canada, 303

Wines of Chile UK Ltd., 296

wine storage, 13, 32, 263–66

wine tasting, 37, 39–46

Winetasting (Broadbent), 296

wine tasting groups, 272

Wirra Wirra Vineyards, 241

Wittmann, 181

Wolf Blass, 236, 241, 289

wood (flavor/aroma), 44, 63, 239

Woodman, Jason, 303

Woodman Wines & Spirits Inc., 303

wood staves, 240

Woodward Canyon Winery, 212, 289

Wyndham Estate, 288

Wynn's Coonawarra Estate, 241, 285

X

Xarel-lo, 9, 156

Y

Yakima Valley AVA, 211
Yalumba, 238, 241
Yamhill-Carlton District, 209, 210
Yarden, 194
Yates-Campbell, Rebecca, 304
yeast (flavor/aroma), 52
yeast, 92, 107, 170, 282
yellow apple (flavor/aroma), 95
Yellow Label Cabernet Sauvignon 2002, 236, 289
[yellowtail], 237
[yellowtail] Cabernet-Merlot 2004, 237
[yellowtail] Cabernet Sauvignon 2005, 237
[yellowtail] Chardonnay 2005, 237
[yellowtail] Merlot 2005, 237
young wines, 30, 33, 47, 49, 262
Y series, 238

Z

Zachys (wine merchant), 274
Zefina, 211
Zind, 103
Zind 2001, 292
Zinfandel, 6, 35, 203, 204, 205, 211. *See also* Prim-
    ivito
Zinfandel Port, 204
Zinfandel Vintners Blend 2003, 288